the BROWNS
Cleveland's Team

RICHARD SHMELTER

SPORTS PUBLISHING INC.   WWW.SPORTSPUBLISHINGINC.COM

Director of Production: Susan M. McKinney
Book design, project manager: Jennifer L. Polson
Cover design: Terry N. Hayden

Photos on pages 1, 5, 7, 8, 10, 11, 12, 15, 16, 19, 21, 36, 40, 41, 46, 48, 52 (John Sandusky), 60, 62, 65, 68, 69, 72, 73, 78, 79, 83, 84, 85, 86, 87, 88, 89, 91, 98, 100, 102, 103, 105, 107, 108, 109, 110, 113, 116, 118, 121, 122, 125, 126, 127, 128, 130, 132, 136, 137, 139, 143, 150, 154, 155, 157, 159, 161, 163, 164, 172, 174, 187 and 195 courtesy of the Cleveland Browns.

Photos on pages 2, 3, 4, 6, 9, 14, 17, 18, 28, 35, 37, 38, 45, 47, 52 (Otto Graham), 54, 56, 101, 156, 162, 166, 180 and 181 courtesy of Ted Patterson.

Photo on page 71 courtesy of the Baltimore Ravens.

ISBN: 1-58261-141-6
Library of Congress Card Number: 99-64801

Printed in the United States.

SPORTS PUBLISHING INC.
804 North Neil
Champaign, IL 61820
www.SportsPublishingInc.com

To my wife Helen, who still seems to love me after all this time.
Also to my mother Arlene, who never stopped encouraging or listening to me.
Finally, in loving memory of my dad and buddy, Joseph Shmelter (1930-1995).
May you shine as bright up in Heaven my dear dad as you will forever in my
heart. I hope you are proud. I know I am for having you as a father.

Acknowledgments

My sincere thanks and appreciation must first go to Mike Pearson at Sports Publishing, Inc. for giving me this opportunity and believing in my manuscript.

My wife Helen must also be acknowledged whenever this project is mentioned. Not only does she have to put up with me on a daily basis, which sometimes can be quite trying, but she also had to be my sounding board, editor, and critic, whether she liked it or not. Through it all, however, she prevailed like so many times before, and for that I will be eternally grateful.

I would also like to acknowledge my fellow co-workers in Cleveland Electric Laboratories' MGO department. Over the course of this project, they listened to my ideas, and gave me encouragement to keep going.

Finally, a grateful thank you must go out to Dino Lucarelli of the Cleveland Browns organization. He allowed my wife and me to come out to the Browns complex and look through his archives for most of the pictures that appear in this book. He truly made the experience one that I will never forget.

Contents

Introduction

Back in 1944, a Chicago sportswriter named Arch Ward had a dream, and thanks to this man of vision, the All-America Football Conference came to be. Along with the birth of this new league, the city of Cleveland, Ohio, began a love affair of over fifty years.

Ward had a knack of developing promotional ideas and turning them into success stories. He was credited with starting the major league baseball All-Star Game, which continues to grow in popularity with the passing of each year. Ward also started the college All-Star football game in Chicago. This was a game that pitted the best of the college seniors against the previous season's NFL champions. The game was played in July or August from 1934 to 1976, and for most of those years, had a huge following.

By 1944, with the All-Star games soaring in popularity, Ward set his sights on another brainstorm. This time he came up with a concept to start a new professional football league consisting of eight teams. His main plan was to have the winner of the new All-America Football Conference play the NFL champion at the end of the season in a football version of the World Series. It looked like a wonderful plan, but sometimes even the best laid plans never come to be.

Unfortunately, the NFL didn't want any part of Ward's plan. The NFL looked at the new league as a second rate collection of castoffs with no talent, and refused Ward's idea. Despite the rude snubbing from the NFL, Ward refused to let his dream die, and on June 4, 1944, the AAFC was born in St. Louis, Missouri, with representatives from Buffalo, Chicago, Cleveland, Los Angeles, New York, and San Francisco in attendance. Teams from Brooklyn and Miami were added later to make up the eight cities. Former Notre Dame player Jim Crowley was named commissioner, and by September, 1946, the All-America Football Conference kicked off its first football season.

The Cleveland franchise was purchased by Cleveland businessman Arthur "Mickey" McBride, who then hired Paul Brown in 1945 as the team's head coach. From there, Brown assembled a team that he himself hand picked. Paul Brown was one of the greatest observers of football talent the sport has ever seen, and over the years, his knowledge would pay off in huge dividends.

With this book, you the reader will be taken through many of Paul Brown's successful moments, as well as those of other coaches and players who were lucky enough to don the orange and brown colors of this wonderful organization. I hope you enjoy reading it as much as I had the privilege of writing it. I also hope that it is the perfect link between a cherished past, and a promising, exciting future as we head into the next millennium.

Richard J. Shmelter
Cleveland, Ohio
July 1999

BROWNS' FIRST-EVER WIN

[SEPTEMBER 6, 1946]

On a hot summer evening one year after the end of World War II, the Cleveland Browns started what would become a 50-year love affair with the city they called home. In front of 60, 135, which was largest crowd to ever witness a pro game in Cleveland up to that time, the Browns kicked off their inaugural season in stunning fashion, winning 44-0 over the Miami Seahawks.

Prior to the opening kickoff, the crowd was entertained by musicians and majorettes performing popular songs of the time period, along with a fireworks show. There was also a time to remember fallen comrades, and for this, the lights of Municipal Stadium were turned off and "Taps" was played while the public address announcer read the names of pro football players who lost their lives during World War II.

Mac Speedie

Cleveland got things going early when local hero Cliff Lewis from Lakewood hit end Mac Speedie from 19 yards out for the first-ever regular-season score in Browns history. The touchdown came eight plays into the game, and was the result of a Mike Scarry fumble recovery on the Miami 29. After Gene Fekete and Don Greenwood ran the Browns to the 19, Lewis found Speedie in the corner of the end zone for the score. Lou Groza's first of five conversion kicks made it 7-0 with only 3:45 expired from the clock.

The Browns got the ball back quickly after the defense stuffed Miami, and forced them to punt on fourth down. Groza then booted the first of many field goals throughout his career from 22 yards out to end the first quarter with Cleveland up, 10-0.

Gaylon Smith

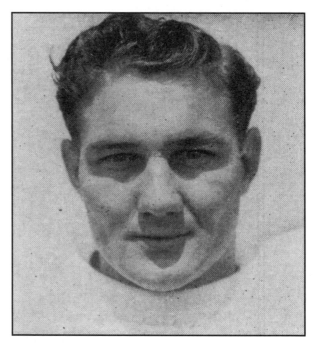

Gene Fekete

Midway through the second quarter, the Browns struck once again through the air. With Otto Graham now at quarterback, Cleveland went 80 yards in six plays for their second touchdown.

Dante Lavelli teamed up with Graham for two key plays in the short drive. The first came on third down from the Cleveland 21 after two passes only netted one yard. Graham then found Lavelli for 25 yards to keep the drive alive. Three plays later, following a 17-yard run by Gaylon Smith, Lavelli caught a pass on the Miami 2 and scored with ease. Groza's extra point made it 17-0.

The Browns made quick work of the Miami defense once again on their next possession. On the first play of the drive, from midfield, Graham threw to halfback Tom Colella. The fleet-footed Colella caught the ball behind the line of scrimmage, then sprinted up the middle of the field without much trouble. Within sec-

onds he crossed the goal line, and with Groza's extra point, the Browns were in complete control, 24-0.

Things continued to go bad for the Seahawks when quarterback Jim Tarrart fumbled for the second time deep in his own territory.

From the Miami 34, Gaylon Smith, who was on his way to leading all ball carriers in the game, took the ball and barreled straight up the middle for another quick score.

For the first time in the game, Miami finally got a break when the Browns were penalized for clipping, but their luck was short-lived. Cleveland got the ball back, and Groza ended the first half with a 20-yard field goal to give the Browns an almost invincible 27-0 bulge at the intermission.

After a scoreless third quarter, the Browns rang up another score early in the fourth. On third down from the Miami 3,

OFFICIAL PROGRAM 25c

BROWNS
VS.
BROOKLYN
DODGERS
OCTOBER 6TH, 1946

CLEVELAND STADIUM

Don Greenwood

Don Greenwood's alertness counted for six points when he scooped up Lou Saban's fumble and ran across the goal line.

After Groza made the score 37-0 with his third field goal, the huge crowd had seen enough and began to leave with extreme confidence in their new football team. Just when the crowd thought there was nothing left to cheer about, defensive back Ray Terrell proved them wrong.

In one final desperate attempt to get some points on the board, Walt McDonald let loose with a long pass that Terrell intercepted on the Cleveland 24. He then took off down the sideline, and didn't stop until he scored the final touchdown of the game just as the clock hit zero. Groza added his fourteenth point of the game, and Cleveland completed their 44-0 demolition job on the Miami Seahawks.

The Cleveland Browns played a perfect game in their debut. They rolled up 314 total yards while allowing just 22. The Seahawks only managed to cross midfield once in the entire game. The Browns were definitely for real, and looked to build on their spectacular start. And what a start it was.

BROWNS WIN 1946 AAFC CHAMPIONSHIP

[DECEMBER 22, 1946]

Just to prove that their opening night performance was no fluke, the Browns proceeded to wreak havoc on their next six opponents. With the passing of Otto Graham, the power running of Marion Motley, and a tenacious defense, Cleveland rolled over Chicago, Buffalo, Brooklyn, Los Angeles, and New York twice, by a margin of 136 points to 35. After that they hit a snag and lost two straight, then ended the season with five straight wins to finish first in the Western Conference with a 12-2 record. In those last five games, the Browns outscored the opposition 207 to 52.

The man responsible for putting together this fantastic team was head coach Paul Brown. Brown had a keen eye for talent, and hand picked each player on the Cleveland roster. With their success, the Browns led the AAFC in attendance with an average of 60,000 per home appearance.

On the field, Cleveland was led by quarterback Otto Graham, who finished the season as the AAFC's second-ranked passer. He threw for 1,834, and his 17 touchdown passes led the league.

Helping to make Graham's job a lot easier was the AAFC's top receiver, Dante Lavelli. He caught 40 passes for 843 yards, which were both tops in the

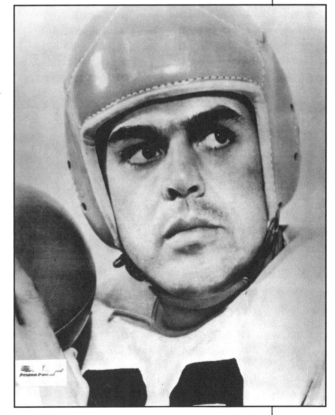

Otto Graham

league. The ground game was led by bruising fullback Marion Motley. The Browns also had the league's leading scorer in Lou Groza, who lived up to his nickname " the toe", by kicking for 84 points. With all this talent, it shouldn't come as a shock to know that the Browns produced a league-high 423 points.

Cleveland's opponent for the first-ever AAFC championship were the New York Yankees, who won the Eastern Conference with a 10-3-1 record. Led by head coach Ray Flaherty, the Yankees put together a championship-caliber team with a mixture of old NFL players and young rookies.

The old pros who took over leadership were quarterback Ace Parker and tackle Frank (Bruiser) Kinard. Parker was 34 years old and in his final pro season, but was still a standout triple-threat ball handler. He was also one of the best defensive backs to ever play the game. Kinard provided solid blocking on the offensive line and anchored the defensive line with tough tackling. His 1946 season was so successful that he became the first ex-NFL player to earn a spot on the AAFC all-pro team.

The leading rookie on the Yankees was Spec Sanders. He developed into an all-around talented player, and led the league in rushing (709 yards), and rushing touchdowns (six). He threw for 411 yards and four touchdowns, and also caught 17 passes for another three scores. Sanders was also a tremendous special teams player, averaging 15 yards on punt returns and 30 yards on kickoffs.

On December 22, 1946, the Browns hosted the first AAFC championship game in front of 41,181. The temperature was 32 degrees at kickoff with snow falling throughout the game.

The Browns received the opening kickoff, but turned the ball over

quickly when Graham was intercepted at midfield.

On New York's first offensive play, Sanders ran for no gain. He then had a pass deflected. After those first two plays, coach Flaherty replaced Sanders with the veteran Parker, and things got going for the Yankees. Parker quickly got New York down to the Cleveland 7, which was close enough for Harvey Johnson to give New York a 3-0 lead with an 11-yard field goal.

Cleveland made some noise following the ensuing kickoff when Graham connected on a screen pass to Edgar Jones, who turned the play into an 82-yard touchdown. The play was called back to the Cleveland 35, however, because an official claimed that Jones stepped out of bounds along his way down the sideline after picking up 17 yards.

Graham continued to attack through the air, hitting Mac Speedie twice and Lavelli once. The Browns stalled once

Edgar Jones

Dante Lavelli

1946-49 Cleveland Browns

they reached the New York 3, and on fourth down, Paul Brown decided to go for a touchdown instead of a field goal. When Graham dropped back to pass on fourth down, he was sacked for a loss of 13, and the first quarter ended with New York holding on to their slim three point lead.

The Yanks were stopped following their brilliant goal line stand, and were forced to punt. After Graham returned the punt to the Cleveland 30, he went right to the air with deadly accuracy. He connected on seven straight passes to get the Browns to the New York 13. Cleveland then switched to their power running attack. On two straight carries, fullback Marion Motley first plowed up the middle to the 1, then capped the drive off from there. With Groza's extra point, the Browns took a 7-3 lead into halftime.

The Browns' momentum continued early into the third quarter when John Yonakor recovered a fumble on the New

York 36, but Groza missed a 42-yard field goal four plays later to kill the drive.

New York took over possession on their 20 following the missed field goal. Parker started the series off with two straight pass completions to John Russell that got the Yanks to the Cleveland 42. New York shifted over to their ground game, and it proved just as successful. Parker and Sanders took turns running, and got the Yanks to the Cleveland 2. From there, Sanders put New York up, 9-7, with a run up the middle. Harvey Johnson was considered automatic on extra point tries during the season, but his streak of 36 straight came to an end when he missed on the conversion.

The Browns got to the New York 12 on their next series thanks to Motley's 51-yard run, but Groza once again missed an easy field goal attempt. His woes continued a short time later when a 37-yarder went wide. New York got lucky when Groza missed those two field goals, and with eight minutes remaining in the game, they looked to run out the clock.

From his 20, Sanders got things going with a breakaway 25-yard run. The Yanks bogged down from there, and Parker decided to punt on third down, with the logic being to pin the Browns deep in their own territory with very little time left.

The Browns took over on their 24 following Parker's kick. Motley started the series off with a pickup of 10 yards. After Edgar Jones gained a yard, and Graham missed on a pass attempt, the Browns found themselves in a critical third-and-nine situation. Graham dropped back on third down looking for his money receivers, Speedie and Lavelli, but both were well covered. He then spotted Jones cutting across the middle, and threw a bullet to him. The pass was low, but Jones showed exceptional athletic ability by bending down to catch the ball at the shoe tops while running full speed. He gained 24 yards on the play, and gave Cleveland new life at the New York 42.

Graham got tricky on the next play by lateralling to Lavelli, who then did the same to Don Greenwood, who faked out the defense for a gain of eight. Graham lateralled again on the following play, this time to Tom Colella to get the ball to the 16. From there, Graham dropped back into the pocket looking for Lavelli, who broke off the line and was running straight for the end zone. Lavelli then cut sharply to the right as Graham's pass hit him right on the numbers at the 6. The defender

Tom Colella

covering Lavelli made a diving attempt to knock the ball away, but all he got for his effort was a face full of mud. Lavelli crossed the goal line untouched, and Groza's conversion gave the Browns a 14-9 lead with 4:13 left in the game.

The Browns refused to be over-taken at this stage. They flexed their de-fensive muscle and stopped New York from coming even remotely close to threatening their lead. As the final gun sounded, the city of Cleveland had their second straight pro football championship. In 1945, the Cleveland Rams won the NFL championship before moving to Los Angeles. Cleveland was, and still is, the only city that can boast of winning back-to-back football titles in two different leagues.

BROWNS WIN 1947 AAFC CHAMPIONSHIP

[DECEMBER 14, 1947]

Once again the Browns and Yankees

dominated their conferences, with Cleveland finishing at 12-1-1 under Paul Brown, while New York went 11-2-1 with Ray Flaherty at the helm.

This was the season in which quarterback Otto Graham came into his own as one of pro football's elite signal callers. He ruled all AAFC passers in 1947 by completing 163 passes out of 269 attempts for 2,753 yards and 25 touchdowns. All those figures led the league, and Graham was the unanimous choice for AAFC Player of the Year.

Mac Speedie led the league in both receptions (67), and receiving yards (1,146), while Dante Lavelli chipped in with 49 catches for 799 yards and 9 touchdowns. Marion Motley led the ground attack with 889 yards, and Edgar Jones' 6.4 yards per carry was the best in the league.

The title game rematch between the Browns and Yankees took place in New York's Yankee Stadium with 61,879 in attendance. The field was half frozen, but with temperatures in the 40s, the remaining ice started to melt, which made for a muddy mess throughout the afternoon.

New York received the opening kickoff, but gave away possession after three downs. Cleveland didn't fare much better, and the game started to show signs of becoming a punting exhibition in the early going.

Cleveland came to life after returning a punt to their 33. On second-and-seven, Graham faked a handoff, then flipped a long lateral to

Marion Motley

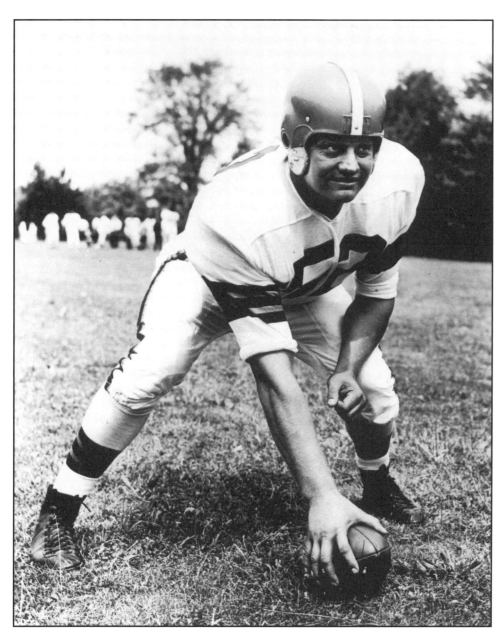

Frank Gatski was a center from 1946 to 1956.

Motley's brilliant run almost went for nothing, because on the next play Graham was intercepted. Lady Luck shined on the Browns, however, as the Yankees were penalized for defensive holding prior to the pass. Cleveland continued to have possession, and following a pass to Speedie that put the ball on the 1, Graham scored on a quarterback sneak to give the Browns a 7-0 lead.

New York countered with an impressive drive of their own following the kickoff. With Spec Sanders and Buddy Young ripping off huge gains on the ground, the Yanks got to the Cleveland 5. From there, the Cleveland defense stiffened, and Harvey Johnson salvaged the drive with a 12-yard field goal to make it 7-3.

The Browns used a ball-control attack to eat up the remaining time left in the first half. They did have two opportunities to blow the game wide open, but penalties nullified one touchdown and took them out of range after they reached the New York 6.

Motley. The powerful fullback blasted off tackle, and after getting up a full head of steam, he cut to the middle. He blew by ten defenders while cutting back toward the sideline, then was tripped up after Harmon Rowe managed to get a hold on one of his feet. Motley couldn't keep his balance for long ,and eventually fell to the ground on the New York 13 after gaining 51 yards.

The second half started off the same way as the first did, with both teams exchanging punts for a while. The Browns then got a break on one punt when Bob Kennedy's kick went out of bounds on the New York 43 to give Cleveland excellent field position. Unfortunately, the Browns lost the ball quickly when Edgar Jones fumbled on the New York 37.

The Yankees' offensive unit was barely on the field thirty seconds before they returned possession back over to the Browns thanks to a Tom Colella interception.

From the New York 41, Motley once again ignited the Cleveland offense with a 16-yard gain up the middle. Graham then connected on two straight passes that got the Browns to the 6. On third-and-goal from the 4, Graham faked a lateral to Motley, and once the defense was sucked into thinking he had the ball, Graham slipped a handoff to Jones, who went into the end zone untouched. Lou Saban's extra point gave the Browns a 14-3 lead at the end of three quarters.

All throughout the final quarter, Cleveland's defense continued to beat up on the Yankees. The closest they got was the Cleveland 19, but Buddy Young fumbled from there, and Lou Saban re-

Lou Saban

covered to kill the drive. The Browns ran out the clock from that point on, and made it two-for-two in AAFC title games.

The Browns were starting to show that they were a team that could compete with the best in the NFL, but the other league was still not impressed with their abilities. Within a year, however, the Browns would prove to the entire football community that they were definitely a force to be reckoned with.

BROWNS BECOME FIRST TEAM IN PRO FOOTBALL HISTORY TO GO UNDEFEATED

[1948]

The NFL's Chicago Bears came close twice, in 1934 and 1942, but lost out on undefeated seasons in the championship game both times. Until 1948, the Bears were the only team to even get that far when it came to going unbeaten throughout an entire season. A team needs to be extremely talented, injury free, and have luck on their side from time to time to even come remotely close to perfection. In 1948, the Cleveland Browns were that team, and over the course of 14 games plus the championship contest, they became the first organization to reach perfection.

The road to Cleveland's dream season began on September 3 against the Los Angeles Dons at home. With 60,193 in attendance, the Browns took a 19-0 lead into the fourth quarter despite having a sluggish offense throughout the game. The Dons did rally for two late touchdowns to make it 19-14, but their final score came with only five seconds remaining, which wasn't enough time for them to try for the win.

On a trip to Buffalo, the offense woke up for one of its best showings during Cleveland's AAFC days. With a well-balanced attack, the Browns rolled, 42-13. Otto Graham threw for two scores, and ran for another. Marion Motley carried 17 times for 136 yards and a touchdown, while Mac Speedie tied an AAFC single-game record by catching 10 passes, with one going for a score.

Even though the Browns won big, 28-7, over the Chicago Rockets in week three, it was a very physical game. The Rockets keyed on Motley all day, allowing him just 49 yards on the ground. With his running game shut down, Graham took control through the air, and threw for three touchdowns. He also accounted for Cleveland's other score with a 12-yard run in the first quarter.

Chicago came to Cleveland the following weekend for a rematch, and gave the Browns an early scare. Taking advantage of a sputtering Cleveland offense, the Rockets jumped out to a 10-0 halftime lead. It

was once again Graham who came to the rescue. After having his problems in the first half, Graham found the mark with his passes, and connected with Bill Boedeker from 37 yards, and Dub Jones from 43 yards, to put the Browns out in front. Boedeker added the clincher in the fourth quarter on a 2-yard run to give Cleveland a 21-10 win.

On a muddy field in Baltimore, Cleveland had to rely on their ground game to come through. After being shut down over the last two games, the backfield came alive when it was needed most and outrushed Baltimore 226 yards to 84. Motley had 130 yards, while Edgar Jones ran for 61 yards and scored both Cleveland touchdowns in a 14-10 win.

In what looked like a laugher on paper, the undefeated Browns played host to the winless Brooklyn Dodgers on October 10th. As the game progressed, however, the Browns found nothing funny about the Dodgers. Brooklyn gave them one heck of a game, and were tied 17-17 going into the final quarter. One of the bright spots for Cleveland during this tough battle was when Lou Groza kicked a record 53-yard field goal in the first half. The Browns caught a break from the pesky Dodgers early in the fourth when Ray Ramsey fumbled on the Brooklyn 12, and defensive end George Young grabbed it and scored to break the tie. The Browns added

George Young

another touchdown to make the final 30-17 after Motley capped off a time-consuming, 17-play, 73-yard drive with a run from the Brooklyn 3.

On the third play of the next game against Buffalo, Edgar Jones caught a perfect pass from Graham, and went 35 yards for a touchdown. The Browns never looked back from there, and coasted to a 31-14 victory after two hard-fought contests. Graham threw for two more touchdowns, while Motley ran for one, and Groza added a field goal.

Dante Lavelli returned to the starting lineup for first time in 1948 after being sidelined with an injury. With his favorite receiver healthy once again, Graham exploded for 310 yards through the air on 21 out of 30 attempts and 4 touchdowns. In the 35-7 whipping of the New York Yankees, Lavelli caught two of Graham's touchdown tosses.

Scoring a touchdown in each quarter, the Browns beat Baltimore, 28-7, for their ninth win of the season. Edgar Jones scored twice, while Motley and Ara Parseghian added the others.

On November 14th, Cleveland Municipal Stadium was the site of the AAFC's battle of the unbeatens. A crowd of 82,769 packed themselves into the stadium to set the then all-time pro football attendance record. Led by quarterback Frankie Albert, the 49ers were the Browns' equal during the 1948 season, and came into Cleveland with a 10-0 record, and averaging 426 yards total offense per game.

On the third play of the game, with just 45 seconds removed from the clock, Graham scored from 14 yards out to put the Browns up, 7-0. San Francisco came right back to tie it on a Joe Perry 3-yard run. From then on this game became a tough defensive battle. Edgar Jones managed to break the tie following the second-half kickoff by finishing an 84-yard drive with a run off tackle from the 3. The Cleveland defense then took over, and completely shut down the 49ers. They allowed the explosive 49ers just 185 total yards, intercepted Albert four times, and didn't allow them to cross midfield throughout the entire second half. With their 14-7 win, the Browns were now atop the Western Conference all by themselves.

In a hard-hitting affair against New York, the Browns managed to explode in the second quarter to break a 14-14 deadlock, and get out of Yankee Stadium with a 34-21 win. The hitting was so intense that four Cleveland players had to leave the game with injuries. Thankfully, Marion Motley stayed healthy, and carried the offensive burden. He scored Cleveland's first touchdown after catching a Graham pass, then went 78 yards for the score. He added a 12-yard touchdown run in the third quarter to close out the Browns' scoring. On the day, Motley averaged over 7 yards per carry, and finished with 75 yards.

In Los Angeles four days later, the Browns had to come from behind twice to win, 31-14 over the Dons. After being held scoreless in the first quarter, Graham rallied the Browns by throwing two touchdowns and scoring one himself. He suffered a severely twisted knee in the fourth quarter, but it didn't turn out to be

Lou Groza

a season-ending injury. Tony Adamle also scored a touchdown, and Lou Groza added a field goal in the Browns' 12th win of the season.

The Browns completed a grueling three-games-in-seven-days trip with a Western Conference clinching win over the 49ers. Tired and banged up, the Browns trailed 21-10 in the third quarter before coming to live. Up until the opening kickoff, it was uncertain whether or not Graham would be able to play. Graham decided to give it a try, and limped out for the Browns' first series. He looked like the Graham of old despite his pain, and put Cleveland in the lead quickly with a 41-yard touchdown pass to Lavelli.

After San Francisco went up by eleven points, the Browns showed true fighting spirit by not allowing themselves to be tired and sore. They sucked it up like the champions they were and scored three touchdowns over the last eight minutes of the third quarter to win, 31-28. Graham was the true warrior on this day, and with his knee throbbing in pain, he led his team to victory by throwing three touchdown passes in the third quarter. On the receiving end of his scoring strikes were Marion Motley, Dub Jones and Edgar Jones.

In the regular season finale, the Browns built up a 31-0 lead by the third quarter before leaving Brooklyn with a 31-21 victory. Graham completed 10 out of 17 passes for two touchdowns, and also ran for one. Motley balanced the offensive attack out with 88 yards on the ground.

Not only did the Browns dominate their opponents throughout the season, but they also led the way when individual honors were given out. Otto Graham walked away with the most honors. His 2,713 passing yards led the league, and his 52 percent completion rating was good enough for third place in that category. He was selected all-pro, and was co-winner of the AAFC Most Valuable Player award with San Francisco's Frankie Albert.

Also topping the league from the

Bill Willis

Browns were Marion Motley's 964 rushing yards, and Mac Speedie's 58 receptions. Both were unanimous choices for all-pro, as were Dante Lavelli, Lou Rymkus, Bill Willis, Ed Ulinski, and Lou Saban.

The Browns' quest for perfection never hit any snags in the championship game, as they blew past the Buffalo Bills, 49-7 on a day that saw Motley run for 133 yards on 14 carries for a tremendous 9.5 yard per carry average, and two touchdowns. His performance was so dominating that he outrushed the entire Buffalo backfield twice over.

Lou Rymkus

Eddie Ulinksi

And so it was over, and the Cleveland Browns of 1948 became the first pro football team to ever go through an entire season undefeated. The Browns brought an end to the most magical year that ever was in Cleveland sports history. In the spring, the Cleveland Barons won the American Hockey League championship in convincing style. As spring turned to summer, the Cleveland Indians won a tight American League pennant race, then beat the Boston Braves in the World Series. By the end of the calendar year, the Browns gave the city its third championship with a perfect 15-0 record. It also marked their 18th win in a row over two seasons, and their 24th straight without a loss.

BROWNS WIN FOURTH STRAIGHT AAFC CHAMPIONSHIP

[DECEMBER 11, 1949]

By 1949, the All-America Football Conference was all but finished. With Cleveland's complete domination of the league, interest in the AAFC began to dwindle. To put it simply, the AAFC was too much Cleveland Browns. They were so perfect that they became almost predictable. Because of this, attendance around the league began to go down, and combined with travel expenses and salary wars with the NFL, the league was all but through as the 1949 season grew near. At the end of the season, the AAFC announced that it was folding, and would merge with the NFL starting in 1950.

Coming as no surprise, the Browns were once again the elite of the league in 1949. Along the way to another conference title, however, they showed the world that they were human after all. After extending their winning streak to 29 straight games, the Browns got pounded by the San Francisco 49ers, 56-28. They did get over the crushing defeat by going on to win five out of their remaining six games while tying the other, to post a near perfect 9-1-2 record.

There was a new playoff system in effect for the AAFC's final season. The format called for the team who finished first in the standings to play the fourth-ranked team. The other game pitted number two against three. The winners of those games would then meet for the title. The Browns gained their berth with a 31-21 win over Buffalo, while San Francisco defeated New York, 17-7.

The San Francisco 49ers could have been the best team in the history of the AAFC if not for the Browns. They had just as explosive an offense as Cleveland, and in 1949 they rang up a league-high 416 points on their way to a 9-3 finish.

For the third time in four years, the Browns hosted the AAFC championship game. On December 11th, before a small crowd of only 22,550, and on a field made up of snow and slush, the Browns and 49ers battled it out for the final AAFC crown.

Cleveland received the opening kickoff, and started throwing right away. Despite their aggressive opening attack, they didn't produce a sustained drive and had to punt.

The Browns regained possession after the 49ers also had trouble moving the ball. From his own 43, Graham found Speedie for 38 yards on the first play of the new series. Five plays later, Edgar Jones ran off the left guard hole from two yards out for a touchdown that gave the Browns a 7-0 lead going into the second quarter.

Throughout the first quarter, the 49ers played very conservatively by keeping the ball on the ground the entire time they had possession. Frankie Albert then opened things up with a pass to Alyn Beals for nine yards. That completion got the 49ers in gear, and they advanced to the Cleveland 24. The Browns stopped the 49ers' assault from there, with Horace Gillom sacking Albert for a loss of ten yards on third down. Joe Vetrano tried a field goal attempt from 41 yards, but it fell short.

After both teams took turns punting, the Browns had the ball on their 37. Graham went to his running game after a first-down pass fell incomplete. On second-and-ten, Graham spun and tucked the ball into Motley's midsection. The power back then tore straight up the middle with his legs pumping. He hit top speed once he was past the line of scrimmage. With Lavelli running interference for him, Motley made his way through the San Francisco secondary with the speed and power of a locomotive. Lowell Wagner managed to catch Motley inside the 10, but paid dearly for his effort as all he got was a

straight arm blast from the fullback. Motley went untouched the rest of the way to complete his 63-yard run. Groza's conversion made the score 14-0 going into the final quarter of AAFC football.

San Francisco began a long march near the end of the third quarter, and finished it off in the fourth when Albert threw to Paul Salata for a 23-yard touchdown that cut the Browns' lead to 14-7 following Vetrano's conversion.

If the 49ers had any visions of grandeur, the Browns quickly ended them with an 11-play, 67-yard drive after Salata's touchdown. The final touchdown in AAFC history came at 6:13 of the fourth quarter when Dub Jones ran off right tackle from the San Francisco 4. Groza added the final point, and Cleveland clinched their fourth straight AAFC title, 21-7.

The history of the All-America Football Conference was all Cleveland, as their 52-4-3 overall record will testify to. The Browns were now ready to take their act into the NFL.

Otto Graham in a crowd of well wishers.

BROWNS' FIRST NFL WIN

[SEPTEMBER 16, 1950]

Officially, the first Super Bowl was played in January, 1967. Unofficially, one can go back to late summer of 1950 for its conception. For on the evening of September 16, 1950, the four-time AAFC champion Cleveland Browns met the two-time defending NFL champion Philadelphia Eagles in the first game of the season.

After the merger of the two leagues became official, NFL commissioner, Bert Bell, thought that scheduling the season opener between these two champions would bring more fans over to professional football. It would also bring an end to a four-year feud between the two leagues over who was the supreme ruler of pro football.

Back in 1944 when the AAFC was founded by Arch Ward, this was what he had in mind. Let the winners of the AAFC play the NFL champions for the ultimate prize, which is how the concept of the Super Bowl came to be in the mid-sixties. Unfortunately, the NFL was not that open-minded in the mid-forties. They thought that they were kings of their domain, and scoffed at the idea that any other league could even come close to being their equal.

Most NFL owners didn't even give the Browns credit when they won all four AAFC titles.

Despite the talents of Cleveland's head coach and players, the NFL's top brass still claimed that the Browns were champions of a second-rate league, and that the worst NFL team could whip the Browns. They just didn't see the Browns as anything but a laughingstock, and looked forward to the day when the mighty Philadelphia Eagles would give them an old-fashioned butt whipping to finally put the second raters in their place.

The NFL owners had reason to be cocky when bragging about their chances against the Browns. The Philadelphia Eagles were loaded with talent, and had just come off their second straight NFL championship, both of which were won by shutouts. They were led by coach Earl

(Greasy) Neale, who within a few seasons, took the Eagles from doormat to one of the greatest teams ever assembled in NFL history.

Their main weapon was running back Steve Van Buren. Entering his seventh season in 1950, Van Buren set the stage for all future runners to follow. He was the first running back to have both speed and power, and he used both equally well, and much to the chagrin of opponents. His glory years were from 1947 to 1949, in which time the Eagles won three divisional titles and two NFL crowns. In that time period, Van Buren won three NFL rushing titles, set the single-season record of 1,146 yards, and set an NFL championship game record by running for 196 yards against the Los Angeles Rams in 1949.

Tommy Thompson

Coupled with Van Buren, Neale also had all-pro tackle Al Wistert, another tough runner in Bosh Pritchard, quarterback Tommy Thompson, future hall of fame end Pete Pihos, plus many more. To put it in simpler terms, the Eagles were loaded with talent on both sides of the ball.

Despite all that Neale could be proud of, it was his defense that seemed to give him his greatest thrill. It was a 5-2-4 alignment dubbed the "Eagle Defense". Prior to the 5-2-4, most NFL teams used a 5-3-3 alignment, which consisted of five down linemen, three linebackers, and three defensive backs. This setup worked great to stop the running game, which was the main weapon of attack prior to 1940. After that, most teams realized the importance of a passing game, and attacking the 5-3-3 became an easy task, seeing that there were only three defensive backs to cover the passing lanes. Neale saw what was happening, and came up with a solution. He took out one of his linebackers and replaced him with a fourth defensive back.

The purpose of the "Eagle Defense" was to slow down the passing game, but still be able to apply pressure on the quarterback and stop the running game. At the snap, the five down linemen would charge in while the linebackers bumped the receivers to slow them up. The secondary then had four fast backs who could keep up with the swift receivers, and the Eagles had the number-one secondary in the NFL. They lacked size, but made up for this with speed and toughness.

Over the course of the three previous seasons, Neale's defense terrorized ninety percent of their opponents, and when the defense was through, Neale would then send his Van Buren-led offense onto the field to kick you some more. Ah yes, Greasy Neale and company did have it made in the later forties, but that was about to change as the new decade of the 1950s came along.

Once Paul Brown knew that his team was going to merge with the NFL, he set out to study all he could about the teams he would soon be facing. He started with the Eagles, seeing that he knew they would be Cleveland's first-ever NFL opponent. He dissected the famed "Eagle Defense", and saw that its armor could be pierced after all.

Brown saw the famed defense was effective when opposing teams were lined up in a tight formation, but could be hurt severely by using a halfback as a man-in-motion, and spreading wide receivers, Mac Speedie and Dante Lavelli, out at the far end of the line of scrimmage. This alignment filled the "Eagle Defense" with holes. It forced the two linebackers to make the decision of either covering the flats against a pass to the ends, or protecting the middle of the field against the run or screen pass over the middle. The Philadelphia secondary was ranked number one in the league, but Speedie and Lavelli had great speed, which in time could wear down even the best when trying to cover them on every down. In this case, the linebackers would be forced to help out in the coverage of the two ends, thus leaving the entire middle open for the power running of Marion Motley to run through, or Otto Graham to pass to any number of talented teammates. To make matters worse for the Eagles was the fact that their famed defense was the only alignment used, so if an opponent started beating up on it, there wasn't much that could be done.

The Browns experimented with their game plan throughout the preseason, and with devastating results. They ran up 175 points on their way to a perfect 5-0 record. On top of that, they worked on it every day in training camp. To say that the Browns were ready for their NFL debut would have been an understatement.

In the past, if the "Eagle Defense" did run up against some trouble, the explosive Philadelphia offense was usually there to put enough points on the board for a win. That was, however, when the offense had all their main weapons healthy, which was not the case prior to the opening game against Cleveland.

The first, and most important member of the Eagles' offense, Steve Van Buren, went down with an injured toe during a 17-7 loss to the College All-Stars in early August. It continued to hamper his running so much that he was forced to miss the entire preseason. Also forced to watch from the sideline were halfback Bosh Pritchard (shoulder injury), and star tackle Al Wistert (knee injury).

Even though most of the sports fans in Philadelphia were caught up in a hot pennant race involving their Phillies at the start of the 1950 NFL season, a crowd of 71,000 took time away from baseball to pack themselves into Philadelphia Municipal Stadium on Saturday night, September 16th. It would have been a safe bet to say that not many of the 71,000 in attendance gave the Browns a chance to even score, let alone win. Confidence ran high as the huge throng entered the stadium, but despair would be there to greet them on their way home.

The Eagles got first crack at the ball, but failed to move it and punted on fourth down. Joe Muha punted to Don Phelps, who shocked the crowd with a 64-yard return for a touchdown. The stunned crowd then began to cheer when the officials brought the play back due a clipping penalty. The Browns not only lost

Jim Martin

out on a score in the first minute, but suffered an even greater blow when star tackle and kicker Lou Groza went down with an injured shoulder while blocking on the Phelps punt return. The place-kicking responsibilities were then taken by Chubby Griggs, who hadn't kicked on a regular basis since high school.

The Browns failed to move the ball after the penalty, as did the Eagles on their next possession. Once again Phelps took a Muha punt and ran through the Eagles' coverage team with ease. He was stopped this time, but not before he advanced the ball 46 yards. Once again, however, Phelps' hard work went for nothing, as another clipping penalty nullified a great return. While reviewing the films of this game, Paul Brown and his staff could not see where the clipping occurred on both of Phelps' returns. It seemed that even the officials were against the Browns on this day, but it could never be proven.

As the first quarter was narrowing down, the Eagles mounted a good drive with runs to the left side of the Cleveland line. A Thompson to Pihos pass completion then got them to the Cleveland 9-yard line. That was as far as the Eagles got

on this drive thanks to a tough defense that might have bended but not broken. Philadelphia had to settle for a 15-yard field goal by Cliff Patton to give the Eagles a 3-0 lead.

After receiving the ensuing kickoff, the Browns only managed to get one first down, and were then forced to punt. Thanks to a lucky break, they got the ball back quickly. Horace Gillom got off a high kick on fourth down, and as Clyde Scott attempted to field the punt on the run, he lost control of it and fumbled. Jim Martin quickly recovered it for the Browns on the Philadelphia 39.

Graham looked to capitalize on Scott's error, and hit Speedie with a 19-yard completion on first down. The drive stalled from there, as Cleveland could only muster three yards on the next three downs. Griggs then came in to try a 25-yard field goal that would have tied things up, but his lack of kicking experience showed when his attempt missed by a mile.

The Eagles took over on their 20, but failed to move the ball, and Muha's fourth-down punt sailed out of bounds on the Cleveland 41.

Don Phelps

From this point on, the Browns proceeded to kick the two-time defending NFL champions all over the field. It first appeared that the Eagles were getting the best of the Browns, but Paul Brown and company were just waiting for the right time to unleash their arsenal.

Throughout the early stages of the first quarter, the Eagles seemed to think that they had Cleveland's game plan read pretty well. Whenever Rex Bumgardner went in motion from his half-back position, the defense shifted its coverage over to that side of the field, which left all-pro defensive back Russ Craft alone in his coverage on one of the receivers split wide. At this time it was Dub Jones who Craft was covering, and living up to his all-pro status. What the Eagles didn't know, however, was that Jones was just toying with Craft. He wanted Craft to believe that he was doing a good job in his coverage, and when the time was right, Jones would go full speed at Craft and surprise him.

Following an offside penalty, Paul Brown felt that the time was right to open up his offense, and allowed Jones to stop acting the part of a well-covered receiver. At the snap, Graham took a short drop, while Jones faked to the outside. Jones then turned on the speed, running past the shocked Russ Craft, who never had

Cliff Lewis

time to get started. Behind great protection, Graham sent a pass in Jones' direction that he caught in full stride at the 25-yard line. With the nearest defender five yards off the pass, Jones had no trouble completing the 59-yard scoring play. Griggs had better luck with his kicking foot on the extra point attempt, and Cleveland was out in front to stay as the first quarter came to a close a short time later.

The Browns were having trouble establishing a ground game throughout the first half, and two Marion Motley fumbles didn't help matters. Both came as the Browns were driving, but thanks to great defensive efforts, the Browns were able to come away unharmed.

Cliff Lewis played a major role in one of those great defensive efforts when he intercepted a pass on the Cleveland 29. Graham then hit on three passes, and Motley redeemed himself with a fine 15-yard run, to get the Browns to the Eagles' 26. From there, Graham called on Dante Lavelli. At the snap, Lavelli did a spin move on linebacker Alex Wojciechowicz, then shook free from safety Frank Regan with a fake to the outside. The result of this play was another easy pass completion for a touchdown, as Lavelli caught Graham's pass all alone under the goal posts. With Griggs' extra point, the Browns took a 14-3 lead into the locker room at halftime.

Cleveland received the second-half kickoff, and within five plays, the Browns covered 79 yards for another score. Graham hit on all five pass attempts in this short drive. The first three went to Bumgardner, who was now driving the "Eagle Defense" crazy with his man-in-motion moves. Lavelli was next, and he responded with a 32-yard gain, which put the ball on the Philadelphia 12. Graham decided it was time to get his other receiver, Speedie, in on the scoring, and got off a good pass despite being in the clutch of two defenders. Speedie made a leaping catch on the 2, and fell in across the goal line for the touchdown. Griggs connected once again on the extra-point try to make it a 21-3 game at the end of three quarters.

The Eagles cut the lead to 21-10 when Pete Pihos caught a 17-yard touchdown pass from Bill Mackride. That score did nothing to dampen Cleveland's spirit, and the Browns responded by scoring two more touchdowns before it was all said and done.

Throughout the first three quarters, the Browns ran only ten times, but at this stage of the game, Graham looked to the ground attack to run off as much time as he could. He told his linemen to spread out a little more at the line of scrimmage. When the Philadelphia defensive linemen saw this, they naturally lined up nose-to-nose with the man across from them. This move helped the Browns get better angles on their blocking, and with that, the field was now wide open. Motley, Jones, Bumgardner, and Graham then began to punish the Eagles with good gains. Graham carried seven straight times on one drive, with the finally one going for a score from the 1-yard line.

The Browns then added one final nail to the Eagles' coffin a short time later. After Jones rapped off a huge 57-yard gain on the ground, Bumgardner ran in from the 1, thus giving the Browns their fifth touchdown of the evening. Griggs was now in the kicking grove, and ended the scoring with his fifth extra point, to make it a 35-10 thrashing.

Otto Graham received a huge trophy for being named the "Outstanding Player of the Game". He hit on 21 passes for 346 yards and three touchdowns. Even though Graham got the trophy, everyone on the Browns deserved a small piece of it. They executed their game plan perfectly on offense, while the defense held the explosive Eagles to 266 yards total offense.

The Browns' first NFL victory was so brilliant that it prompted a visit to their locker room by NFL commissioner Bert Bell, who told Paul Brown and his men that they were the best team that he had ever seen. The other teams in the NFL would also follow Bell's sentiment by the end of the season, whether they wanted to or not. The Browns were just that good.

official souvenir program

25¢

Football's Greatest Year

cleveland

BROWNS

NATIONAL FOOTBALL LEAGUE

VS.

Chicago CARDINALS

OCTOBER 15th 1950

For the BEST in SPORTS..

Read the Cleveland **Press**

BROWNS WIN AMERICAN CONFERENCE PLAYOFF

[DECEMBER 17, 1950]

Despite their whipping of the invincible Philadelphia Eagles, the Browns were still having trouble getting respect around the league. Many felt that if the Eagles had all their top performers healthy, they would have taken the Browns. With the way that the Browns played on that evening, it was highly unlikely that anyone could have beaten them, but it made for good conversation among the Cleveland haters. As the season wore on, coaches across the NFL would call each other about how to stop the new kids from taking over the neighborhood. They even sent their game films to each other in hopes of finding some flaw somewhere that could bring down this new juggernaut. In today's game, films of opponents are sent each week to coaches, but in 1950, it was not practiced. It even seemed that the officials were calling penalties where there were none, but through it all, the Browns hung tough and continued to grow as a unit. They also became more determined to prove the football world wrong.

The Browns finished the regular season with a 10-2 record, as did the New York Giants. In fact, the only blemishes on the Browns' record were given to them by the Giants. New York was coached by a crafty man named Steve Owen, who had been involved in pro football since its early days as a player and coach. He was New York's head man since 1931, and could match wits with the best of them, which he proved in his first two meetings with Paul Brown.

Owen and his top scout had watched the Browns' win over the Eagles, and went to work on a way to stop their offense. What they came up with was a 6-1-2-2 alignment, also called the "Umbrella Defense". It called for six linemen, one linebacker in the middle, and four defensive backs. The trick of this defense was that the ends would drop off into pass coverage to protect the flats, while the backs would spread out to cover more of the secondary. It gave the Giants seven men who could now cover the fast and talented Cleveland receivers. From up in the press box, the formation looked like an umbrella according to sportswriters, so the name stuck. This formation was later modified into the 4-3 defense which is used today.

In the Browns' two regular season meetings with the Giants, the new defensive alignment completely baffled Graham. In their first meeting, the Browns were shut out for the first time in their history, 6-0. Three weeks later, they lost 17-13, and their only touchdown came after a botched kickoff return was recovered on the 5-yard line. Graham scored the touchdown, and Groza added two field goals.

After the second New York game, Paul Brown was worried that the Browns had hit their peak to early and were on the way down. His players restored Brown's confidence by then going on a six-game winning streak to finish out the year. Unfortunately, the Giants refused to go away, and stayed step by step with the Browns down to the wire. With both teams finishing in a dead heat, a special playoff game was set for Sunday, December 17, in Cleveland.

The day of the game dawned bone-chilling cold, and didn't improve as the day wore on. By game time, the temperature was 10 degrees, and a powerful wind off Lake Erie swept through the open end of Municipal Stadium to make it seem even colder to the 33,054 brave-hearted fans. With the field resembling an ice rink, both teams decided to wear tennis shoes for better footing.

Just like the two regular season meetings, this game was a defensive battle from the opening whistle to the final gun. The teams only crossed midfield a total of three times throughout the game. The Giants never got there until the first play of the fourth quarter, and Cleveland man-

aged it twice, and capitalized on it each time.

The first time Cleveland crossed midfield was right after the opening kick-off. Things looked easy for the Browns on this drive, as they seemed to have the "Umbrella Defense" finally figured out. The Giants seemed to differ, and once the Browns reached their 7-yard line, the New Yorkers tightened down. From there Groza gave the Browns a 3-0 lead with a field goal. The slim lead that the Browns had after their opening drive held up until the halfway point of the fourth quarter.

After almost an entire game of brutal defensive stands, the Giants finally were the first ones to break loose. Thanks to three future hall of famers on Cleveland's side, however, New York didn't get to celebrate that long.

The first hall of famer to step up in the final ten minutes was middle guard Bill Willis. Willis was having a great game up to this point, but will forever be remembered from this game due to one huge play. A quick halfback named Charlie Roberts took a handoff from Charlie Conerly, and raced around the right end. He broke into the clear, and appeared to be home free for the go-ahead score. With the way this game was being played, it could have been the winning score. Seeing the urgency of what was about to happen, Willis took flight after the swift Roberts. Despite being 215 pounds, Willis could move. He was an accomplished sprinter throughout high school and college, and needed every bit of that training to catch Roberts. With every muscle pumping, Willis took off in pursuit. After covering 32 yards, Roberts was caught from behind by Willis on the 4.

Willis wasn't done there. On the

next two plays, he stopped Eddie Price for no gain on two runs up the middle. Conerly went to the air on third down, and found Bob McChesney for a touchdown, but an offside penalty saved the Browns. Conerly went back to the pass, but this time Tony James intercepted, only to have his effort go for nothing due to a defensive holding penalty. After the ball was moved half the distance to the goal line, Price ran to the 3. On second down, Willis was once again the man, as he broke through the line to drop Joe Scott for a loss of ten yards. Jim Martin then batted down a Conerly pass, and on fourth down Randy Clay tied the game at 3-3 with a 20-yard field goal.

With 6:10 remaining in the game, Dominic Moselle returned the ensuing kickoff to the Cleveland 35-yard. This is where the second future hall of famer did his part for the Browns. With New York keying on the league's rushing champion, Marion Motley, Graham carried the ball three times on this drive for 36 yards. On first down he went right up the middle for nine yards. After Bumgardner picked up a first down on the next play, Graham went off tackle for 15 yards to move the chains deeper into New York territory. On second down from the 38, Graham faked a handoff, spun through the middle, and was finally stopped on the 26-yard line. After two penalties and a tough defensive stand, the Browns faced a fourth down with 58 seconds left in regulation.

At this time, Cleveland called on the third future hall of famer to do his part. Willis held the Giants for the offense. Graham then got the offense deep enough for a field goal attempt, and it was now time for Lou (the toe) Groza's turn. The ball was spotted on the 29-yard line, and Groza set himself up for the chance to put the Browns into the title game. Throughout this game, Groza played his tackle position with a tennis shoe on his left foot, and a square-toed football shoe on his right one minus the cleats for when he had to kick. It might have looked odd at first, but nobody rooting for the Browns seemed to care when his famed kicking foot sent the ball sailing over the uprights to give Cleveland the 6-3 lead.

The Browns couldn't rest on their laurels just yet. They had to make one final defensive stand to assure a trip to their first NFL title game. It didn't take them long, however, to begin a victory celebration. Bill Willis once again came through. This time he led a trio of Browns through the line in hot pursuit of Conerly. The quarterback had no where to go, and eventually succumbed to Willis in the end zone for a safety. The Browns got the ball and just the final seconds off the clock to preserve their hard-fought 8-3 victory.

Over in the National Conference, the Los Angeles Rams and Chicago Bears had also finished in a tie at the end of the season with 9-3 records. The Rams had it a lot easier than the Browns in their play-off game, winning by a more comfortable score of 24-14.

The 1950 season was one of the most exciting throughout the history of the NFL, especially for Browns' fans. Both conferences went down to the wire, and for the first time in pre-Super Bowl days, playoffs were needed to determine who went to the championship game. The excitement didn't stop there, because the NFL title game was yet to be played, and it proved to be just as heart-stopping as the conference races were.

BROWNS WIN 1950 NFL CHAMPIONSHIP

[DECEMBER 24, 1950]

The climax to the 1950 NFL season couldn't have been scripted any better by a Hollywood screenwriter. Here you had the upstart Cleveland Browns about to play the team that they replaced five years earlier in the hearts of football fans throughout the city.

After the Cleveland Rams won the NFL title in 1945, owner Dan Reeves decided to move his team to Los Angeles. The Rams never drew big crowds in the four years that Reeves owned the team. They also were not that good, which could explain the lack of interest by the majority. Still, the Rams were all that Cleveland had at the time, and the true football fan was glad to have them, even if they were the minority.

In 1945, the Rams drafted a young, gifted future hall fame quarterback out of UCLA named Bob Waterfield, and their luck changed overnight. The Rams went from doormats to the jewels of the NFL by posting a 9-1 record, and beating Washington, 15-14, for the championship. Waterfield's exploits on the field made all the difference, as he ran, passed, and kicked his way to earning the NFL's Most Valuable Player award.

The Rams' good fortune on the field didn't carry over to the turnstiles. Despite their performance, they only drew a total of 73,000 for four home appearances. Reeves knew that he had to do something, and after only 32,178 came out to see the championship game, his decision came swiftly. In defense of the fans, the temperature that day was barely above zero. One must remember that people didn't have the cold weather apparel in 1945 like they do today, so sitting outside at that time in those conditions was pretty much unheard off. In any case, by the middle of January, 1946, Reeves announced that he was moving his team to Los Angeles.

The Rams flourished on the west coast, and by 1950, they were one of the most explosive teams offensively to ever set foot on a field.

They were still led by Bob Waterfield, but he had to share the quarterback duties with second-year man, Norm Van Brocklin. Head coach Joe Stydahar used whoever had the hot hand at the time. At the end of the season, the Rams rewrote the NFL record book for most points in one game (70), points scored in one season (466), passing yards (3,709), total yards as a team (5,420), and touchdowns scored (64).

Los Angeles was blessed with five players who ran the 100-yard dash in under 10 seconds. The fastest of the five was former Heisman Trophy winner, Glenn Davis. A talented, all-around athlete, Davis led the Rams in rushing with 416 yards, and caught 42 passes out of the backfield for another 592 yards.

Joining Davis in the backfield on a regular basis was power back Dick Hoerner. Just like at the quarterback position, Stydahar also rotated his backfield whenever the need called for it. When he wanted speed, Stydahar called on Davis, but when he needed brute force running, he went to his "Elephant Backfield" of Deacon Dan Towler and Paul Tank Younger. Both men were 6-2, and over 220 pounds, and brought a whole new meaning to the term power running.

When the Rams needed yardage through the air, they had two future hall of famers to throw to in Tom Fears and Elroy (Crazylegs) Hirsch. Fears caught 84 passes to lead the league in that category for the third straight season. Hirsch chipped in with 42 receptions of 687 yards.

It shouldn't come as a shock to find out that the Rams were the number-one ranked offense in the league, and they would get their biggest test of the year when they came to Cleveland to play for the championship against the top rated defense.

In Los Angeles, the weather is almost always sunny and dry. Unfortunately, the 1950 NFL championship game was scheduled to be played in Cleveland on December 24. Cleveland is a wonderful city, but its winter season can be nasty at times, and the week prior to the title game was one of those times. Throughout the week, the field at Municipal Stadium was frozen, but the temperatures managed to get high enough to melt the ice. Then it rained, and once again got cold. By game day, the temperature was at a chilly 29, with a cold wind swirling around the stadium. The field was by no means perfect, but it was a lot better than when the Browns played New York on it the previous weekend for the American Conference title. Due to the cold conditions, the Browns only managed to get 29,751 to come out for their first shot at the NFL crown.

The Browns won the coin toss and elected to kick off. After the Rams returned the kick to their 18, Bob Waterfield came out to start the game at quarterback. Van Brocklin was scheduled to start, but an injury in the playoff game with Chicago forced him to the sideline.

As Waterfield observed the Cleveland defense, he noticed the Browns were in a 5-3-3 alignment. This meant that the Browns only had three defensive backs in the secondary, and Waterfield looked to take advantage of it early. Sending one man in motion to the right, Waterfield sent the much-feared Tom Fears across the middle. With Cleveland's attention focused on Fears, Glenn Davis slipped out of the backfield virtually unnoticed. Linebacker Jim Martin was assigned to cover Davis, but he went over to help cover Fears, which left Davis in the open down the sideline at the Rams' 45. Waterfield jumped at the opportunity presented to him, and hit Davis with a perfect pass. Davis then used his sprinter's speed to complete the one-play, 82-yard drive. The game was only 27 seconds old as Waterfield kicked the extra point to give the Rams a very quick 7-0 lead.

Not to be outdone, the Browns came right back within six plays to tie it at 7-7. Graham started it off with a run of 21 yards. He followed that up with three pass completions, with the final being a tremendous 31-yard diving catch in the end zone by Dub Jones. Groza added the conversion.

With two high-powered offensive teams on the field, scoring points is a given. This game proved it, because Waterfield took the Rams on an eight-play drive right after Cleveland's touchdown to regain the lead. The drive consisted of two key plays. The first one was a 44-yard pass from Waterfield to Fears which got the Rams deep into Cleveland territory. Vitamin T. Smith then accounted for the other by exploding around the left end for 15 yards down to the 5. Fullback Dick Hoerner capped the drive by slamming his massive 6-4, 220 pound frame into the end zone from three yards out. Waterfield's conversion made it a 14-7 game at the end of the wild first quarter.

One of Cleveland's plans against the Rams called for the running backs to run wide out of the backfield at the snap. This plan would force the linebackers to run toward the sidelines to cover the backs. This left a void in the middle of the field.

Receivers Mac Speedie and Dante Lavelli were being covered one-on-one, and as mentioned earlier in this book, it was hard to keep up with them in man-to-man coverage. With the linebackers out of the picture most of the time, the cornerbacks had no help if Speedie or Lavelli got away from them across the middle.

When the Browns got the ball back, Graham set out to attack the opening over the middle. From the Cleveland 35, Graham sent Speedie and Lavelli deep. He threw to Speedie across the middle, but the pass fell incomplete. The Browns were helped on the play by a pass interference call on defensive back Woodley Lewis. Graham went back to Speedie, and this time the all-pro receiver hung on to the ball for a gain of 17. With the ball on the Los Angeles 26 following Speedie's catch, Graham once again sent his backs out toward the sidelines. The linebackers took the bait, and this left Lavelli in lone coverage by Tom Keane. By the time Graham dropped back, Lavelli had already shook off Keane and was open down the middle. The result was an easy 26-yard touchdown for "Glue Fingers" Lavelli.

On the extra point try, the snap from center was too high for holder Tommy James to get at. He couldn't get it down fast enough for Groza to try the kick, and with the Rams coming in on him, he decided to pick up the ball and run or pass for the extra point. He spotted Tony Adamle, and threw it toward him. Adamle had a hold of the ball for a split second, but lost the grip.

That completed the scoring in the first half, and thanks to that high snap, the Rams were up, 14-13, at the intermission.

In the early minutes of the third quarter, the Rams concentrated on their ground game. It looked to be successful, as the Rams wore down the Cleveland defense with run after run until they reached the Browns' 7-yard line. The Rams then got sloppy. Vitamin T. Smith was called for holding, and then Waterfield was intercepted by Ken Gorgal to kill an excellent drive.

The Browns couldn't take advantage of the turnover, and gave the ball back to Los Angeles after three downs. Gillom helped aid the Rams by shanking his punt. The ball only traveled nine yards, and gave Los Angeles possession at the Cleveland 46.

The Rams once again drove deep, getting to the 12. From there, the Browns allowed only four yards to be gained on them. On fourth down, Waterfield dropped back to attempt a chip shot field goal from 15 yards out. Waterfield had been one of the most accurate field goal kickers in the NFL, but this time he proved to be human after all. He hit the ball wrong, and the kick sailed wide of its mark.

Ken Gorgal

The Browns took advantage of their good fortune by going 77 yards on five plays for the go-ahead touchdown. Once again it was Lavelli who delivered the blow, this time catching a 39-yard pass from Graham on the 8 and going untouched into the end zone. This time the snap from center was perfect, and Groza nailed the extra point to give the Browns a 20-14 lead.

After blowing two scoring opportunities with an interception and a missed field goal, Waterfield was determined to get the Rams back in front. At first the going look tough, as Cleveland flexed its defensive muscle.

After missing most of the season with a broken jaw, Len Ford was ready to get back into action, and that spelled bad news for the Rams. Unable to eat due to his injury, Ford lost 15 pounds, and was not back to full strength. From early on, the Rams were eating rookie defensive end Jim Martin alive with good gains to his area. Paul Brown felt that despite his inactivity, Ford could shut the Rams down on his side of the field. Even though he wasn't 100%, Ford played like he never missed one down during the year.

Ford made his presence felt immediately by disrupting the Rams' attack to his side of the field. On one series, he personally accounted for 38 yards in losses. On first down, he stopped Smith for a 14-yard loss while he was trying to run a reverse. After sacking Waterfield for 11 yards, Ford ended the series by dropping Davis for 13 more while he was attempting to sweep the end.

The Rams managed to adjust to Len Ford's presence toward the end of the third quarter, and within a span of twenty-five seconds, they scored two touchdowns to go into the fourth quarter leading, 28-20.

The tying touchdown came on a Hoerner 1-yard blast after the power back carried seven straight times from the Cleveland 17. Waterfield's conversion then broke the tie. After the kickoff, the Browns began on their 20. On the first play, Graham pitched out to Motley. The fullback swept the right side and picked up eight yards, then found himself trapped by most of the defense. He started to run backwards with hopes of finding another opening. As he backpedaled, he lost control of the ball and fumbled. The loose ball hit the ground once, bounced into the hands of defender Larry Brink at the 6, and he went untouched for the score.

The Browns got a much-needed lift five minutes into the fourth quarter when Warren Lahr intercepted Waterfield on the Cleveland 35. Graham was having a great day, but it was on this drive that he seemed to have the most control and poise. He began by attacking the middle for seven straight completions to Lavelli, with one of them keeping the drive alive on fourth-and-four. He saved the drive himself a few plays later by running for a first down on fourth-and-three. Graham finished the drive off with a 19-yard touchdown pass to Rex Bumgardner, who made a beautiful, diving catch in the end zone right before the ball hit the ground. Groza's extra point then made it a 28-27 Rams' advantage with 4:35 left in the game.

With three minutes remaining, Tommy Thompson intercepted Waterfield to give the ball back to Graham. With momentum on his side, Graham drove the Browns inside the Los Angeles 30. On third down, Graham called a quarterback

Len Ford

draw. He broke free from a group of defenders, tucked the ball, and after getting the needed yardage, set his sights on the end zone. As he crossed the 20-yard line, linebacker Milan Lazetich blasted him from the blind side, and while going down, tried to stretch out for extra yardage and lost control of the ball in the process. The Rams recovered with three minutes left to play, and a devastated Graham made the long walk to the sideline feeling that he just cost the Browns the championship.

Paul Brown quickly found his dejected field general. After putting his arm on Graham's shoulder, Brown told him not to worry, that he would get one more chance at winning the game. After all, Cleveland had the number-one ranked defense, and there was still plenty of time left. That conversation seemed to lift Graham's spirits a bit, but the defense still had to stop the Rams for him to get his chance at redemption.

Rex Bumgardner

From this point, the Rams were just looking to run out the clock. With the two-minute warning coming up, Waterfield looked to keep the ball on the ground. Twice he handed off to Hoerner, but the defense stopped him for no gain both times. Davis did a little better with a run off right tackle, but came up short of a first down by four yards.

With under two minutes to play, Waterfield was forced to punt from his 30. Aided by a strong wind, he got off a spec-tacular 51-yard kick that Cliff Lewis caught on the 19, and advanced to the 32-yard line with 1:50 left.

With the wind at his back, and 68 yards in front of him, Graham was once again confident and ready to give Cleveland an NFL championship.

The Rams were now looking for Graham to pass on virtually every down, so they plugged the passing lanes with everyone they could. Unable to find an open receiver on first down, Graham ran the quarterback draw, but this time he held onto it. The result was a 14-yard pickup out to the Cleveland 46. Los Angeles was now forced to keep some players up close to the line of scrimmage after Graham's productive gain. This in turn loosened up the pass coverage, and Graham didn't waste any time attacking it.

Bumgardner was Graham's first target, and his reception out of the backfield was good for 15 yards, and put the Browns on the Los Angeles 39. Next it was Jones out of the backfield who Graham connected with for 16 more. With one minute left, the ball was on the 23.

Graham went right back to the air, with Bumgardner making the catch at the 11. Graham then called a timeout to find out what Paul Brown wanted to do with 30 seconds remaining. The ball was marked on the left hashmark after Bumgardner's catch. Brown knew the it would come down to a field goal, and looked to give his kicker the best possible

Hal Herring

Warren Lahr

angle for his attempt. With the wind swirling around the open end of the stadium, Brown felt that the ball should be marked toward the middle of the field. From where the ball now rested on the left hashmark, Brown and his coaching staff were afraid that kicking into the right to left crosswind from that angle would throw the ball off course. With that in mind, Brown called for Graham to run the ball himself one more time toward the center of the field. Graham held onto the ball for dear life, ran to the right, and got the ball positioned in the center of the field at the 9-yard line with 28 seconds to go.

After calling a timeout, Graham came off the field with the crowd now in a frenzy. It was at this time that all the attention in the massive lakefront stadium shifted over to the right foot of Lou Groza. Groza calmly dropped back from his tackle position while waiting for the field goal unit to assemble on the field. The kick would come from the 16-yard

line, and toward the open end of the stadium. Thanks to Graham's final run putting the ball in the center of the field, the wind would not make a difference.

Surprisingly, the mood in the Cleveland huddle was calm. It seemed that everyone just felt that Groza would come through. Despite all the optimism, Groza still had to kick the ball through the uprights. At the snap, center Hal Herring got the ball off perfectly. With tremendous blocking up front, holder Tommy James received the ball and put it down cleanly. The NFL's top kicker then made his approach and hit the ball dead on. The second his foot hit the ball, Groza knew that he got off a beauty. So did James, because he was jumping up and down in celebration, long before the referee signaled that the kick was good. After a few seconds, the referee made it official, and the Browns were up 30-28, with just a few ticks left on the clock.

Norm Van Brocklin came into the game to try a long pass with the hope of a big gain or a pass interference call. Neither happened, as Warren Lahr came up with his second interception of the game.

Pandemonium then became the order, as frenzied Browns Backers roared onto the field. Groza barely managed to make it to the locker room entrance in one piece, as everyone on the field wanted to get at him. In the locker room, Groza's teammates all huddled around him to give thanks to his kicking ability. Some even went so far as to kiss his kicking shoe. Some time later, a friend of Groza's bronzed the famous shoe for him.

This game went down in professional football history as one of the greatest championship games ever played. It was a tremendous finish to a tremendous season.

As for the Browns, they silenced all the doubters who never gave them a chance against even the worst NFL team in head-to-head competition. Yet here they were, champions of the same league who laughed at them for four years. They had truly arrived as a team of greatness, and counting the Cleveland Rams NFL title in 1945, the Browns gave the city of Cleveland six straight professional football championships. No city before or since has ever come close to that record, and it is doubtful if any one ever will.

DUB JONES SCORES SIX TOUCHDOWNS IN ONE GAME

[NOVEMBER 25, 1951]

Dub Jones

Paul Brown was regarded as one of the best assessors of talent in the history of professional football. One just has to look at Dub Jones for one sample of the genius that was Paul Brown.

Born in Arcadia, Louisiana, Jones went on to fame at Tulane University as a football and track star. He was a tall and lanky 6-4, 200 pounder who got the nickname, "Six O'Clock", because he looked like the hands of a clock striking six when he stood up. Jones began playing pro ball as a defensive back with the AAFC's Miami SeaHawks in 1946, and finished out that season with the Brooklyn Dodgers. While playing with the Dodgers in 1947, Jones caught Paul Brown's eye as a player with incredible talent, and it didn't take Brown long to get him into a Cleveland uniform.

After the 1947 season, Cleveland owned the rights to Michigan's All-American halfback, Bob Chappuis. Paul Brown then traded Chappuis' draft rights to Brooklyn in exchange for the 24-year old Jones.

Once in Cleveland, Brown decided that he wanted Jones on offense, and it was there that he would flourish over the course of eight seasons. With his size, he made for an excellent receiver. Brown used him mostly as his man-in motion out of the backfield, and he proved to give opponents fits with his running and pass catching abilities. While Jones went on to help the Browns win five championships in his stay in Cleveland, the All-American that he was traded for only lasted two nonproductive seasons in the AAFC.

Not only did Dub Jones help Cleveland capture championships, but he also helped himself to a piece of one of the most difficult NFL records to obtain.

On the afternoon of November 25, 1951, the Chicago Bears came to Cleveland Municipal Stadium with a 6-2 record, and were in a hot National Conference race with Los Angeles and Detroit. They were a physical team, and capable of giving any team a beating. Cleveland on the other hand was cruising to another American Conference title, and came into the game with seven straight wins. This

Ken Carpenter

game had all the makings of a classic slugfest, but in the end it proved to be just the opposite, as Cleveland completely dominated the Bears, 42-21. The game wasn't even as close as the score makes it appear, because Chicago scored their last two touchdowns after the game was well out of reach.

Not only was the game out of reach for the Bears on this day, but so was Dub Jones. Over the course of sixty minutes, Jones ran and caught his way through the rugged Chicago defense and into the record books by scoring six touchdowns. With those six touchdowns, Jones tied Ernie Nevers' 1929 record, which was also set against the Bears while Nevers was a member of the Chicago Cardinals. In 1965, Gale Sayers of the Bears joined Nevers and Jones in the record book by

scoring six touchdowns against the San Francisco 49ers.

Ken Carpenter got Jones started on his way to the record book by returning a punt 49 yards to the Chicago 34 on the last play of the first quarter. The road to the record book hit a brief snag when Graham was sacked three times during the drive. Cleveland then got a reprieve when Chicago was called for roughing the kicker on fourth down. The Browns quickly moved from the Chicago 48 to their 2-yard line on long runs by Jones and Carpenter. From there, Jones went off left tackle for his first score.

Cliff Lewis gave possession right back to the Browns with an interception. After two penalties against Cleveland, Carpenter ran for 24 yards. From the Chicago 34, Graham called on Jones as a receiver out of the backfield. After getting a jump on defensive back John Lujack, Jones made an easy catch for his second touchdown.

The Browns got the ball back once again by way of an interception, this time from rookie Don Shula in the third quarter. After marching 69 yards down to the 12, Jones took a handoff and went wide around the left end for his third touchdown.

After the Bears scored their first points to make it a 21-7 game, they kicked off to Ken Carpenter, who made his way 48 yards upfield and into Chicago territory. The Bears were penalized an additional 15 yards on the play for unnecessary roughness, which gave the Browns a first down on the Chicago 27-yard line. On this scoring play, Jones made short order of the Bears by taking a handoff on first down and swept the left side. Once around the end, he sliced back toward midfield and headed straight for the corner of the end zone.

Forty seconds into the final quarter, Jones struck for the fifth time by sweeping the right side and scoring from 42 yards out. Carpenter helped get things going on this drive with a fine run that covered 30 yards.

The sixth and final touchdown proved to be the hardest one to get. It was a long pass from Graham that covered 43 yards, which Jones had trouble locating. It was a quick reaction just as the ball came up on him that helped him stretch his arms out as far as he could to make the catch at the last second.

What a beautiful day it was for Jones. He ran the ball nine times for 116 yards, and caught three passes for 80 more. It is said that records are made to be broken. This statement might hold true 99% of the time, but the fact is that some might never be touched, and the one that Dub Jones shares might be one of the rare exceptions to the rule.

John Kissell
Tackle

Darrell Brewster
End

Ken Carpenter
Halfback

Len Ford
End

Lin Houston
Guard

Otto Graham
Quarterback

Hal Herring
Center

Lou Groza
Tackle

BROWNS WIN 1954 NFL CHAMPIONSHIP

[DECEMBER 26, 1954]

The 1954 Christmas season was in full swing as the NFL's regular season wrapped up on Sunday, December 19th. Once again the Browns were winners of the Eastern Conference, and for the third straight year, the Detroit Lions would be their opponents in the championship game.

If you were a member of the Browns or one of their fans at this time, perhaps the main item on your Christmas wish list would surely have been an NFL championship for the city of Cleveland. Most football players and their fans wish for a title to call their own, but in 1954, the dream of Cleveland owning another NFL crown was just that.

After winning five straight league championships from 1946 to 1950, the Cleveland Browns became the first team in pro football history to lose three straight title games. In 1951, Los Angeles got revenge by beating the Browns, 24-17, in the closing minutes of the game. The Detroit Lions were responsible for Cleveland's next two loses. In 1952, they beat the Browns, 17-7, and in 1953, the Lions squeaked by, 17-16, in the final minute.

Despite their championship game misfortunes in the early fifties, the Browns were an incredible success story, as they compiled a regular season record of 30-6. Despite this, the Browns were being labeled as chokers, which seemed a bit ridiculous considering the fact that they had five championships in their eight seasons of existence up to that time. At the end of the 1950 season, the Browns were looked at as an invincible juggernaut, and three years later, with almost the same group of players, they were now called chokers. It seemed a bit unfair, but in sports, the sad truth is that you are only as good as your last performance, especially in high profile contests.

One team that helped more than any other to make the Browns look bad during this period were the Detroit Lions.

Since the Browns came into existence, they pretty much had their way with any team that crossed their path. That was until they played the

Detroit Lions. Ever since the Browns came into the NFL, the Lions had been their Achilles Heal, beating them seven out of nine times up to the 1954 championship game. Cleveland's lone win came during the 1950 preseason, and they tied once during the preseason of 1953. When it came to regular season or championship games, however, the Lions owned the Browns.

While preparing his team for the 1954 season, Paul Brown didn't concern himself too much with what the experts were saying about his team, or the fact that he couldn't beat the Lions. He had more serious problems to address, with the main one surrounding the quarterback position.

In 1954, Otto Graham was only 32-years old, and still had a few good seasons ahead of him. Despite this, the team's failure in the last three championship games wore hard on him, and tarnished his interest in football. He took the losses personally, especially the 1953 game, in which he had the worst quarterbacking day up to that time in title game history. He also missed his family due to the demand put on him by football. With all that in mind, Graham announced while signing his contract for 1954 that he would retire following the season.

On top of Graham's announcement, Paul Brown also had to contend with the loss of other key personnel before the season started. Guard Lin Houston retired after a solid career, along with linebacker Tommy Thompson, Darrell Palmer, Dub Jones, Bill Willis, and Marion Motley. Jones did come back after missing the game so much, and played for two more seasons. Brown also lost two key

members of his coaching staff in Weeb Ewbank and Blanton Collier. Ewbank went to coach the Baltimore Colts, and Collier took over the head coaching job at the University of Kentucky.

Replacing good people is always a hard task, but Paul Brown succeeded. He added former player Ed Ulinski and Paul Bixler to his coaching staff to replace Ewbank and Collier. As for the players, he placed Tom Catlin at Thompson's linebacker spot, while Mike McCormack took over for Willis, and Herschel Forester replaced Houston at guard.

It took time for the new players to work in harmony, but when they did, the Browns were on their way to a 9-3 record and another trip to the championship game. They started off slow, dropping two of their first three games, then ran off eight straight. On the final weekend, Cleveland's winning streak came to an end thanks to their nemesis, the Detroit Lions. Just like in the 1953 title contest, the Browns were out in front in the closing

Lin Houston

minutes, and once again the Lions won it on a long pass.

Even though the Lions rained on the Browns' parade in the regular season finale, they still had a lot to be proud of. Graham rebounded from his poor showing in the previous championship game to lead the league in passing percentage for the second straight season, and earned his fourth consecutive spot on the all-pro team. Joining Graham on the all-pro team were Lou Groza and Len Ford. Groza earned his place as a tackle, but it was still as a kicker that gave him his claim to fame. He led the league in most field goals made for the third straight time with 16. Ford was the defenses' anchor, and the unit was tops in the league.

John Kissell

There was no doubt that the Browns had jelled into a splendid team in 1954, but they still had to get past the Lions in the championship game to reestablish themselves as a team that was for real, and their chance came on December 26th in Municipal Stadium.

Throughout the season, the weather for a Cleveland home game was bad. It either rained or snowed during their six home appearances. On the day of the championship game, however, Mother Nature must have felt that She owed the city of Cleveland, because by kickoff, the 43,827 spectators were treated to an unseasonably warm day that was full of bright sunshine.

Detroit's Jack Christiansen received the opening kickoff on his goal line to get the third championship game meeting between these two teams underway.

Starting from his own 17 after Christiansen's return, quarterback Bobby Layne handed off to rookie Bill Bowman. It looked like Cleveland was going to be in for another long afternoon as Bowman ran through a huge hole for a 50-yard gain down to the Browns' 33. Just as fast as the Lions struck, that was how fast they faltered, as Lew Carpenter fumbled on the next play and John Kissell recovered for Cleveland.

The Browns couldn't capitalize on the turnover, and Graham returned possession back over to the Lions by throwing an interception to linebacker Joe Schmidt on the Cleveland 35. The Browns lived up to their number one ranking on defense by stopping Detroit cold, but the Lions still managed to salvage the drive with a 36-yard field goal by Doak Walker for an early 3-0 lead.

Billy Reynolds gave the fans something to cheer about on the ensuing kickoff by bringing it out to the Detroit 41. Graham wasted little time getting the Browns moving. Behind excellent blocking, Graham had the time to wait for receiver Ray Renfro to shake double coverage. As soon as Graham saw the swift Renfro break free, he released the ball. Renfro caught the ball in full stride on the 8, and entered the end zone at the 6:10

mark of the first quarter. This game marked Renfro's return after missing six weeks with a knee injury.

From this point on, the Browns never looked back. Six minutes after Renfro's touchdown, Don Paul returned a Layne interception 35 yards to the Detroit 8. After almost losing the ball on a fumble, Graham capped the quick drive off by throwing to a well-covered Darrell Brewster. After Brewster made a great catch at the goal line, he was hit hard, but as he was going down, he lunged for the end zone while dragging a defender. This great extra effort helped put another touchdown on the board, and Groza's conversion gave the Browns a 14-3 lead at the end of the first quarter.

After holding the Lions on their next possession, Reynolds returned a punt 42 yards to give the Browns great field position on the Detroit 12. The Browns made it to the one-foot line as the first quarter ended. Graham finished the drive off on the first play of the second quarter with a quarterback sneak. Groza's extra point made it a 21-3 game. On this conversion, Groza broke Ken Strong's record of nine extra point kicks in NFL championship game history.

The Lions managed to get untracked in the following minutes, and scored on a Bowman 5-yard run. With the extra point, the Lions cut the Cleveland advantage to 21-10, but

that would be all the excitement mustered by Detroit for the remainder of the game.

Later in the second quarter, Mike McCormack snatched the ball from Bobby Layne's hand while he was attempting to pass, and gave the Browns excellent field position on the Detroit 31.

On second down, Graham found Brewster inside the 10-yard line. The ball first bounced off Brewster's hands, then in and out of a defender's. Renfro proved to be in the right place at the right time, because the ball fell into his hands at the 7 for a first down. On second-and-five, Graham kept the ball himself. He ran wide to his right, and leaped over several Lions to get into the end zone for Cleveland's

Mike McCormack

fourth touchdown of the afternoon. That was followed by Groza's conversion, which put the Browns in complete control at 28-10.

Cleveland was throwing all different types of defensive alignments at the Lions, and it had Layne completely frazzled. On one specific play, the Browns used a four man rush while three linebackers dropped off into pass coverage. With four men charging in on him, Layne tried to get off a pass to avoid the sack. He threw into heavy coverage, and the result was a Walt Michaels interception at the Detroit 31.

Ray Renfro was called on by Graham once more. At the snap, Renfro slipped out of the backfield while Lavelli and Brewster were covered by the safetymen. With the safetymen's attention focused on Cleveland's two wideouts, Renfro was able to slip by. He raced toward the sideline, faked out one man by changing his direction to the middle of the field, then blew pass two more defensive backs. Graham's pass was on the way as he broke free from the final two defenders. Renfro made a beautiful catch at the 4 by stretching his arms out in front of him as far as they

Ray Renfro

could extend. He kept his balance long enough to score his second touchdown of the game with the closest Detroit players ten yards behind him. Even with a sore knee, Renfro was still regarded as one of the fastest players of his day. With that touchdown, Renfro tied an NFL championship game record for most touchdown receptions in one game. More importantly was the fact that it helped to increase the Browns' margin to 35-10 at the half.

The second half got underway with Reynolds returning the kickoff to the Cleveland 31, and six plays later they were once again on the board. After throwing to Brewster for 43 yards, Graham finished the drive off with a quarterback sneak from the one-foot line. Groza's conversion made it 42-10, and the Browns were well on their way to ending the Detroit jinx, plus their three-year frustration in the championship games.

After a Ken Konz interception set the Browns up on the Detroit 18, fullback Curly Morrison added another score to Cleveland's total with a 12-yard run. Groza's conversion made it 49-10.

The third period ended with another Detroit turnover just as the Lions were mounting a serious drive. Len Ford put on a fierce pass rush on Layne after the quarterback got the Lions to the Browns' 10-yard line. As Ford was about to crush Layne, he tried to pass. The instant Layne went to release the ball, Ford jumped up and caught it. He took off downfield and made his way to the Detroit 45 before being stopped.

Cleveland's final points came after Layne's sixth interception of the day put the Browns on the Detroit 39. Chet Hanulak started the drive off with a gain of 16 yards up the middle. Reynolds added four yards on the ground, then Graham did something that was not common practice for the Browns.

Paul Brown called all the plays from the sideline, but with a 39-point lead in the fourth quarter, Graham decided to change his coaches' call. He did this because he saw Detroit switch to a defense that he felt could be attacked with a play called to the left side. The quarterback was right in his decision, because Hanulak found a huge hole to run through off left tackle, with the result being a 19-yard touchdown. Groza ended the scoring with his eighth extra point kick to make the score 56-10.

As night began to fall over the city of Cleveland and the clock began ticking down the final minutes, Paul Brown took Graham out of the game. As the legendary signal caller came trotting off the field with victory once again his, he received a standing ovation that shook the rafters of Municipal Stadium. He was also the owner of six new championship game records. His name went into the books for most touchdown runs in one game (3), most touchdown passes in one game (3), most points scored by one player in one game (18), career pass attempts (72), most passing yards (952), and most touchdown passes (8).

With the second most lopsided victory in NFL championship game history, the 1954 Cleveland Browns were once again kings of their domain. It was made even sweeter by the fact that it came against their worst nemesis.

BROWNS WIN 1955 NFL CHAMPIONSHIP

[DECEMBER 26, 1955]

As the defending champion Cleveland Browns went off to training camp in 1955, one familiar face was missing. Otto Graham had stuck to his decision about retirement, and left the game as the greatest passer in the history of the game up to that time. More important than that was the fact that he left as a champion.

With his legendary quarterback now relaxing with his family, Paul Brown turned the offense over to Graham's backup of three years, George Ratterman. Brown still felt that Graham retired too soon, but decided to honor his wishes as long as his team continued to win. After losing four preseason games, however, Brown went to Graham with the hopes of luring him back for one final curtain call. It didn't take much coaxing to get Graham to come back. After all, he was the highest paid player of his time, and that alone must have made the decision a little easier.

With Graham back for one last season, all Brown had to do then was find him a backfield. The Cleveland running game was hit hard in 1955 due to Chet Hanulak and Billy Reynolds both being called up for military duty. Brown wasted little time searching for replacements, and within a short time, he got fullback Ed Modzelewski from the Pittsburgh Steelers, and promoted second-year man Fred (Curly) Morrison to starter. Modzelewski found new life in Cleveland, and responded with a solid season of 619 yards on the ground. Morrison did even better, as he led the Browns' ground attack with 824 yards.

With the running game being so productive, it took pressure off Graham. He attempted the fewest amount of passes in his career. He completed 98 out of 185 attempts for 1,721 yards and 15 touchdowns. He won another NFL passing title, and was selected to his tenth straight all-pro team.

With a balanced offensive attack, coupled with the best defense in the league, the Browns finished at 9-2-1 for an unprecedented tenth straight trip to a league championship game.

With almost the same team that beat the Browns for the championship in 1951, the Los Angeles Rams won the Western Conference title with an 8-3-1 record under first-year coach, Sid Gillman, who was regarded as one of the greatest authorities on offensive football. Under his guidance, the Rams continued to ring up yardage. Norm Van Brocklin was now the number-one quarterback, a position he held since Bob Waterfield's retirement after the 1952 season. Van Brocklin still had Tom Fears and Elroy Hirsch as his receivers, and a rookie speedster named Ron Waller at running back.

On a hot December 26 in Los Angeles, a record-setting crowd of 85,693 were in attendance to watch the 1955 NFL championship game.

Los Angeles took the opening kickoff, and made their way to the Cleveland 24. Van Brocklin tried going for it all from that point, and his pass intended for Skeets Quinlan was intercepted by Ken Konz at the 12.

Cleveland couldn't capitalize on the interception, but a short time later they got close enough for Lou Groza to put Cleveland in the lead, 3-0, on a 26-yard field goal.

Early in the second quarter, Van Brocklin tried going to Quinlan once again, and this time the Browns did a lot more damage after intercepting. Spotting Quinlan on the Cleveland 35, Van Brocklin fired a bullet pass in his direction. The ball hit Quinlan's hands so hard that it bounced in and out of his grasp. Defensive back Don Paul picked the ball out of the air and took off down the sideline. Van Brocklin took off in pursuit, but Paul was

too quick. The result was a record for the longest interception return in championship game history. The 65-yard touchdown, coupled with Groza's conversion, gave the Browns a 10-0 lead.

When the Rams got the ball back, Van Brocklin refused to give up on trying to complete a pass to Quinlan. From his own 33, Quinlan came out of the backfield at top speed, heading straight down the field, and right in the direction of Cleveland's two talented defensive backs, Warren Lahr and Ken Konz. With Quinlan running toward them, Lahr and Konz got mixed up in their coverage, and this allowed Quinlan to blow past them. Van Brocklin's pass fell into Quinlan's hands on the dead run at the Cleveland 30. Lahr did manage to make up ground on Quinlan to tackle him, but it was too late, because the tackle occurred in the end zone. Les Richter closed the gap to 10-7 with his conversion.

Cleveland's offense was starting to have trouble moving the ball, but thanks to their solid defense, Graham and company were able to work through it. If it were not for their great defense, this game might have gotten ugly in a hurry for the Browns against such an explosive team. Instead, Tommy James killed another Los Angeles drive with an interception at midfield.

Graham wasted little time pumping life back into the sputtering offense. As Graham took the snap from center on first down, he saw Dante Lavelli break off the line and head across the middle. While Graham was setting up in the pocket, Lavelli broke into the open and began shouting to Graham to throw the ball. Graham answered his receiver's plea with a perfect pass that landed right in Lavelli's

Otto Graham

Maurice Bassett took over at fullback when Ed Modzelewski was shaken up badly at the start of the second half. When Modzelewski was forced from the game, he was leading the team in both rushing and receptions, but Bassett stepped up right away to fill Mo's shoes.

On two straight carries up the middle, Bassett totaled 33 yards to set the Browns up at the Rams' 23. On third down from the 15, Graham faked a handoff to Renfro, then rolled out to his right. On the 5 he cut around a defender and fell into the end zone. Groza's extra point try put the Browns up 24-7, and on their way to consecutive NFL championships.

Cleveland continued to roll following the ensuing kickoff. On the third play following the kickoff, linebacker Sam Palumbo intercepted Van Brocklin on the Rams' 36. Eight plays later, Graham ran through a huge hole created by tackle John Sandusky from the 1-yard line. Groza's conversion upped the score to 31-7.

By the fourth quarter, most of the 85,000 in attendance had seen enough, and began to exit from the Los Angeles Memorial Coliseum. For those that did

hands inside the Los Angeles 20. Lavelli never broke stride after the catch and scored easily. The extra point by Groza made the score 17-7 at the half.

Cleveland began the second half with Groza missing a 48-yard field goal. The defense was once again brilliant, and gave Graham the ball at midfield after forcing the Rams to punt following Groza's miss.

John Sandusky

stay, they were treated to a bit of NFL history when Graham teamed up with Renfro from 35 yards out for the final touchdown pass of his brilliant career.

With the score at 38-7, Paul Brown took Graham out of the game amidst a standing ovation. It was a real honor to get such an ovation on the road, especially after beating up on the home team in a championship contest. It just went to show how great and admired Otto Graham was, and not only in Cleveland, but throughout the country.

With a fog and light mist rolling into the Coliseum, the Rams produced their only sustained drive of the game. It was capped off by rookie Ron Waller's 4-yard run. With the extra point, the final score came to 38-14.

Cleveland's top-rated defense really lived up to its reputation in this one. The unit put incredible pressure on Van Brocklin throughout the game, and because of it, he threw for seven interceptions. Even though the defense held it together long enough for the offense to get untracked, most of the attention pertaining to this game focused on Graham.

As this game came to end, so did the legacy of Otto Graham. This time his retirement was not put on hold, and just like a hero in a western movie, Graham rode off into the sunset a true champion. In his ten seasons at the helm of the Cleveland offense, Graham guided the Browns to the league championship game every one of those years. This accomplishment alone ranks Graham as the number-one quarterback of all time by many football insiders. It is one record of Graham's which is never likely to fall. He was, and always will be, remembered as a true champion and legend. Thanks for the memories Mr. Graham, they sure were sweet.

JIM BROWN SETS SINGLE-GAME RUSHING RECORD

[NOVEMBER 24, 1957]

Legendary. When one looks up this word in the dictionary, there might as well be a picture of Jim Brown next to the definition. The funny thing is that at the time he was drafted, nobody thought much of him, but it didn't take Jim Brown long to prove to Paul Brown and the rest of the NFL that he was something special.

Jim Brown

It wasn't that the Browns didn't want the talented running back from Syracuse, but their priorities on draft day in 1956 were geared toward a quarterback. Without Otto Graham at the helm, the Browns suffered their first losing season, going 5-7 in 1956. Paul Brown looked to the college draft with hopes of landing a quarterback that he could groom into the next Otto Graham.

The top quarterbacks from the college ranks going into the draft were Len Dawson of Purdue, John Brodie of Stanford, and the 1956 Heisman Trophy winner, Paul Hornung of Notre Dame, and Paul Brown desperately wanted one of these three young men.

Meanwhile, up at Syracuse University, there was a running back named Jim Brown who was convincing a lot of pro scouts that he could make a major impact in the pros. One of those convinced was Browns' chief talent scout, Dick Gallagher. He had seen Brown play three times during the 1956 season, and was convinced that he was the best player in the nation. Gallagher told this to Paul Brown, who still wanted to try for a quarterback come draft day.

The college draft was held on November 26, 1956 following the ninth game of the NFL season. At that point, the Browns were 3-6 and tied with Pittsburgh and Green Bay for the third worst record. With Cleveland ranked so low in the standings, Paul Brown was convinced that he could land one of the top three blue chip quarterbacks.

Seeing that the Browns were tied with two other teams on draft day, a coin toss determined who of the three would pick first. Green Bay won the toss, and also landed the bonus pick, which they used to select Paul Hornung. Cleveland lost their next coin toss to Pittsburgh, thus giving them the sixth overall pick in the draft.

Los Angeles had the worst record, and they kept Paul Brown's hopes alive by taking halfback Jon Arnett of USC. San Francisco was up next, and took away one of the quarterbacks on Brown's wish list by picking Brodie. Green Bay took end Ron Kramer of Michigan next. Pittsburgh was up next, and couldn't decide between Jim Brown or Len Dawson. Paul Brown then saw his dream of getting one of the top quarterbacks in the nation fizzle out when the Steelers took Dawson. Cleveland then selected Jim Brown, and by the second exhibition game of his rookie season, Brown made believers out of everyone. In that game against Pittsburgh, Brown started for the first time. On one play in the third quarter, Brown broke into the secondary, turned on the burners, and scored from 48 yards. Paul Brown took him out of the game, casually walked over to him and told the rookie that he would be the starting fullback from that time on. As noted earlier in this book, Paul Brown was a genius at spotting tal-

ent, and he knew what he had in Jim Brown.

At 6-2, 220 pounds, Jim Brown was a well-rounded athlete whose body was made up of solid muscle. With broad shoulders and powerful legs, he had the power, speed and stamina to carry the burden of the offense. He might not have been the next Otto Graham, but what Graham was to quarterbacks, Jim Brown would become to running backs.

Brown brought a new style of running to the NFL. Most fullbacks went into the defense with legs churning and heads down like a battering ram, and if there was no hole, they would still try to plow through. The old-time fullbacks by and large didn't have blazing speed either. Brown changed all that by taking small steps laterally along the line if there was no opening, and once he found a hole, he exploded through it with sprinter's speed. Brown kept his head up, going into the line leading with his shoulders. When a tackler made his move on him, Brown would drop his shoulder and ram his opponent with it, which usually caused the defender to bounce off. Brown also was able to relax a leg once a defender got a hold on it. Once the defender let up, thinking he had a tackle, Brown would tear away like an escape artist out of handcuffs. Sometimes it took five or more defenders to bring him down, and after that he just kept coming at them, play after play after play.

Jim Brown's first regular season game came against the defending NFL champion New York Giants. In a tough defensive battle, the Browns won, 6-3, and Jim Brown ran for 89 yards on 21 carries. He played a major role in the win by running 15 yards up the middle for a

Jim Brown

first down in the drive that led to the winning field goal by Lou Groza.

Brown kept contributing, and Cleveland kept on winning. He got his first 100-yard game in a 21-17 victory over Washington in week six. He gained 109 yards in 21 carries. Brown was now starting to make people around the league aware of his ability. If Jim Brown had any doubters as to his ability, he gave them one heck of a wake-up call on November 24th against the Los Angeles Rams, who came into this game with a 4-4 record.

Up to the home date with Los Angeles, Jim Brown had gained 532 yards, and the Browns were on their way to reclaiming the Eastern Conference title with a 6-1-1 record. With football fever again spreading in Cleveland, the Browns had their largest home crowd of the year at 65,407, and the largest turnout since 1953.

Things looked good for the Browns going into this game. They were on top of the Eastern Conference by a half game, Jim Brown was running well with consistency, and Tommy O'Connell was surprising everyone at quarterback. O'Connell came to the Browns in 1956, and took over at quarterback after George Ratterman and Babe Parilli fell victim to injuries. Going into the game with the Rams, O'Connell was leading the league in passing percentage, and would finish the year in the top spot in that category. With both Brown and O'Connell doing well, they gave the Browns a well-balanced attack through the air and on the ground.

Lew Carpenter gave Cleveland an early 7-0 lead with a touchdown run in the first quarter, and things looked good for the Browns, even after the Rams tied the game up in the second quarter. It was then that linebacker Larry Morris changed the Browns from well-balanced to one dimensional. Morris broke through on a blitz and sacked O'Connell, dropping him hard on his shoulder. O'Connell was forced to leave due to the injury, and Paul Brown had to go with inexperienced rookie Milt Plum. Due to this, Paul Brown looked to Jim Brown to carry the offensive burden for the rest of the afternoon.

Jim Brown answered the call in record-setting fashion. By the end of the day, he carried the ball 31 times for 237 yards and four touchdowns, to break the single-game rushing record of 223 yards set by Tom Wilson of the Rams. Brown also led all Cleveland receivers with three catches for 21 yards.

Following O'Connell's injury, Brown wasted little time taking control of the offense. From the Cleveland 31, Plum handed off to Brown on a fullback draw. He got hit so hard at the line of scrimmage, that the impact knocked off his helmet. Despite this powerful jolt, Brown kept his senses as well as his balance and took off at full speed to complete a 69-yard touchdown run.

The Rams rebounded from the long run, and managed to contain Brown enough for the rest of the first half to go into the intermission with a 21-17 lead.

Los Angeles extended their lead to 28-17 early in the third quarter after Brown fumbled on the Cleveland 29. Tackle Art Hauser scooped the ball up and ran the distance for the score. It looked like the Rams were heading for an upset victory, but that fumble seemed to ignite the Browns. Over on the sideline after the fumble, Jim Brown was livid with himself, and from that point on he became a determined, one-man wrecking machine.

With the crowd getting behind their team, the Browns scored within minutes. The Rams did manage to hold the Browns on three downs, and forced them to punt. It was here that they made an error which began their demise. As Ken Konz was waiting for the snap on fourth down, someone on the Rams jumped early. The penalty gave the Browns the ball on 48, and Jim Brown took it from there. On second down, he shot through for 33 yards down to the 10, and three plays later, he scored from the 1.

The Rams began their next possession on their 20. On first down, rookie Jon Arnett was knocked back for a loss of 2 yards, then Don Colo sacked Norm Van Brocklin. As he got hit, Van Brocklin fumbled, and Colo recovered for the Browns at the 7. On fourth down from the 1, Jim Brown slammed over the goal line for his third touchdown to put the Browns in the lead 31-28.

Los Angeles tried to stop the Cleveland momentum by creating some of their own, but after driving successfully to the Browns' 45, Bob Boyd lost a fumble to defensive tackle Bob Gain. Ten plays later Jim Brown scored his fourth touchdown, and Cleveland was on their way to victory with a 38-28 lead in the final quarter.

The Rams cut the lead to 38-31 on a 43-yard field goal, but any dreams of a comeback were shattered when Jim Brown got loose on a 46-yard run. He was stopped on the Los Angeles 5, and two plays later, Lew Carpenter took it in to end the scoring at 45-31.

The Browns went on to win the Eastern Conference that year with a 9-2-1 record, but lost to Detroit in the championship game, 59-14. As for Jim Brown, he finished the season with 942 yards to win the league rushing championship, the Rookie of the Year award, *The Sporting News* MVP, he made all-pro, and was selected to play in the Pro Bowl. Jim Brown had definitely arrived, and over the course of the next eight seasons, he would set the new standard for future running backs to follow.

JIM BROWN SETS SINGLE-SEASON RUSHING RECORD

1958

In 1934, Chicago Bears running back Beattie Feathers ran for 1,004 yards to become the first player in history to crack the 1,000-yard barrier. Most football insiders felt that Feathers' accomplishment was one of those rare athletic feats that would never be equaled. No one had ever come close to 1,000 yards before, and it was thought that Feathers' mark would never be broken.

Over the next 13 years, it looked like Feathers' record was one of the untouchables, as nobody got near it. In 1947, Steve Van Buren set the new record by running for 1,008 yards, and to prove that it was no fluke, he did it again in 1949, breaking his own mark with 1,146 yards. Tony Canadeo of the Green Bay Packers also ran for over 1,000 yards in 1949. With the accomplishments of Van Buren and Canadeo, the 1,000-yard mark then became the standard goal for all future running backs to shoot for, not only in the pros, but in high schools and colleges as well.

Even though two players broke the 1,000-yard barrier in one season, it was still not common to see many runners join the elite fraternity. In fact, up until the 1958 season, it was only topped seven times in the history of the NFL. By the end of the 1958 season, however, Jim Brown made breaking the 1,000-yard barrier a common practice all by himself.

The 1958 season opened on the road in Los Angeles. Even though Brown didn't set an NFL record like he did against them the previous year, he did most of the damage to help Cleveland win, 30-27. In the third quarter, Brown took a pitchout, and after running over defensive back Jack Morris, ran 38 yards for a touchdown. Later on, Cleveland was down, 27-20, with the ball on the Rams' 5. Brown took a handoff and went wide. He drew a crowd quickly, but eluded them by hurtling over several defenders to get into the end zone. Groza's conversion tied the score. On the winning drive, Brown ran for 15 yards on the first two carries. Rookie Bobby Mitchell added 22 on the ground, which was followed by two more runs by Brown that got Cleveland to the Rams'

22-yard line with under one minute remaining in the game. With 23 seconds left, Groza kicked a 9-yard field goal to decide to outcome. Jim Brown ended the day with 24 carries for 171 yards and two touchdowns.

At Pittsburgh the following week, Brown ran for 129 yards on 17 carries and three touchdowns in a 45-12 victory. On his first touchdown from 23 yards away, he was trapped on the sideline twice, but refused to go down. In the second half, he broke free on a 59-yard scoring run after six Steelers had a shot at bringing him down. He capped his scoring off with a 3-yard run.

In a wild home opener, Cleveland hung on to beat the Cardinals, 35-28. In this high-scoring affair, the fans were treated to a running clinic put on by Jim Brown and rookie Bobby Mitchell. Mitchell was Mr. Outside, running sweeps around the end. The Cardinals were unable to keep up with Mitchell's speed and paid dearly. He finished the day with 147 yards on just 11 carries. On one of those carries, he broke free for a 63-yard touchdown run. Brown was Mr. inside, crashing

between the tackles most of the time. He also made the Cardinals pay. Setting a team record for most carries in a game, Brown crashed into the line 34 times for a season-high 182 yards, and three short yardage touchdowns. After the Cardinals closed to within seven points, it was Brown's power running that helped kill the clock.

On a beautiful autumn afternoon in Cleveland, the Browns ran their record to 4-0 and a two-game lead in the Eastern Conference with a 27-10 win over Pittsburgh. This win marked the sixth straight

Bobby Mitchell

time that the Browns beat their rivals from Pennsylvania. As in most games throughout his career, Jim Brown was the main weapon against the Steelers. He got the Browns out in front early by taking a Milt Plum pass 27 yards for a score in the first quarter. In the second quarter, he took a pitchout, swept the right side, and was off on a 48-yard touchdown. In just four games, Brown already had 635 yards, and was on pace to crush Van Buren's single-season record of 1,146 yards.

In another wild shootout against the Cardinals, the Browns won their fifth straight, 38-24. Jim Brown was once again magnificent, as he ran for 180 yards on 24 carries and four touchdowns. With Cleveland trailing, 24-17, Bobby Mitchell took a handoff on the Chicago 41 and looked for a hole off tackle. The hole was closed, so Mitchell went looking elsewhere for running room. In his attempt to find a new opening, he ran into quarterback Milt Plum. Not wanting to see the play go for nothing, Mitchell caught a glimpse of Brown standing alone in the backfield. Thinking quickly as defenders were about to converge on him, Mitchell tossed the ball to Brown. Responding like the play was meant to work that way, Brown took the pitchout, cut toward the middle, and outraced the safety for a touchdown. Groza's conversion tied the score. On Cleveland's next possession, Brown put his team in front to stay with a 62-yard run up the middle. His season total was now 815 yards on the ground and 14 touchdowns.

All good things have to come to an end, as was the case with Cleveland's winning streak. With 78,404 in Municipal Stadium, the New York Giants put on great defensive showing in the second half to win, 21-17, after spotting the Browns a 17-7 halftime lead. Jim Brown sparked the offensive attack in the first half. On a third-and-a-foot from the Cleveland 42, Brown went into the line and got the needed yardage for a first down, but kept his legs pumping and broke through the best defense in the league to score from 58 yards out midway through the second quarter. After that it was all New York, and with middle linebacker Sam Huff leading the way, the Giants only allowed Cleveland 27 total yards in the second half. Brown still managed to net 113 yards despite having Huff in his face all day. This game marked the beginning of one of the greatest one-on-one rivalries in pro football history. Brown was the top runner of his time, and Huff the premier linebacker. Both men were determined to outdo the other, and the hitting was intense to say the least. The Giants' win cut the Browns' lead in the conference down to one game at the midway point of the season.

Another crowd of over 75,000 were on hand to see Cleveland rebound from the first loss of the season. They came away disappointed, as the Detroit Lions gave them their worst beating of the year, 30-10. Jim Brown had his worst day up to this point of the season. To most runners, 83 yards on the ground would have been reason to celebrate, but for Brown, it was subpar. For the first time in 1958, he was also denied access to the end zone. Brown did, however, manage to get enough yardage to break the 1,000-yard barrier for the first time in his career.

A trip to the Nation's Capital put the Browns back on the winning track with a 20-10 victory over the Washington Redskins. With the Giants losing their game, the win put Cleveland back on top of the Eastern Conference all by themselves. Like the Cleveland Browns, Jim Brown was on top, but not of the Eastern Conference, but of the football world. With 152 rushing yards in this game, Brown became the new single-season rushing record holder with 1,163 yards. He also scored both Cleveland touchdowns from short yardage. He had a long touchdown run in the fourth quarter, but it was called back due to a clipping penalty.

The Philadelphia Eagles were next on Cleveland's schedule, and they geared themselves up to stop Jim Brown. They succeeded in that department where most had failed, but containing Brown still wasn't enough, and Cleveland won, 28-14. The Eagles held Brown to 66 yards on 20 carries, but they didn't do the same to Bobby Mitchell. In one of the greatest special teams performances in Cleveland history, Mitchell was the difference in an

otherwise evenly matched game. On the opening kickoff, Mitchell raced 98 yards for a touchdown, then followed that up with a 68-yard punt return for another score later in the first quarter. Mitchell's heroics helped keep the Browns atop the conference race with a 7-2 record.

In their rematch with the Browns, the Washington Redskins must not have been happy to be the team that Jim Brown set his rushing record against two weeks earlier. Using a swarming, gang-tackling

Jim Brown

style on Brown, the Redskins were able to give the greatest runner of all time his worst day ever, allowing him only 12 yards on 11 carries. With all the attention on Brown, it freed up halfback Lew Carpenter and quarterback Milt Plum to lead Cleveland to a 21-14 victory. Carpenter gained 95 yards on the ground, and Plum hit on 10 of 19 passes for 219 yards and a touchdown.

You can't keep a good man down, and Jim Brown proved that theory correct by rebounding from his disastrous performance with 138 yards in a 21-14 win over the Eagles.

The win gave the Browns a 9-2 record, and at least a piece of the conference crown going into their season finale against the 8-3 New York Giants.

On the first play from scrimmage against New York in freezing Yankee Stadium, Milt Plum faked a screen pass to Lew Carpenter, then handed off to Jim Brown, who wasted little time running 65 yards for a touchdown. It was Brown's first touchdown in a month, and it gave him 18 on the season, which tied an NFL record first set by Steve Van Buren. On the day, Brown had 148 yards on 26 carries. After that, neither team saw the end zone for the rest of the first half, and

just like in their first meeting, the Browns led at the intermission, this time by a 10-3 margin. The Browns had their chances in the second half to widen their lead, but a fake field goal gone wrong, a fumble, and a bad official's call, allowed the Giants to tie the game up with 10 minutes left to play. After scoring the tying touchdown, the Giants held Cleveland, got the ball back, and in a steady snowfall, Pat Summerall kicked the winning field goal from 49 yards out with 2:07 remaining.

With their 13-10 victory, the Giants forced a tie for the Eastern Conference title, and a week later in Yankee Stadium, they beat the Browns, 10-0, in a playoff for the right to play Baltimore in the championship game.

Despite such a dismal finish to an otherwise great season, Jim Brown established himself as the NFL's premier runner. No one could doubt his greatness, only embrace it. For the 1958 season, Brown ran for an incredible total of 1,527 yards in just 12 games. Imagine what kind of numbers he could have put up with the modern-day 16-game schedule. It was a given that he made the all-pro team and the Pro Bowl. He was also the unanimous choice for the NFL's Most Valuable Player award.

JIM BROWN SCORES FIVE TOUCHDOWNS AGAINST DEFENDING CHAMPION BALTIMORE COLTS

[NOVEMBER 1, 1959]

On December 28, 1958, the Baltimore Colts were forever immortalized in pro football history by winning what was coined, "The Greatest Game Ever Played". Led by former Cleveland assistant coach, Weeb Ewbank, and a cast of future hall of famers, the Colts beat the New York Giants, 23-17, in overtime to win the NFL championship. It marked the first and only time that an NFL championship was decided in overtime.

The Colts of 1959 were well on their way to winning back-to-back championships when they faced the Browns on November 1. They were led on the field by Johnny Unitas. What Jim Brown was to running backs, Unitas was to quarterbacks. He is regarded by many pro football historians as one of the top three quarterbacks of all time. This was the first meeting between the arm of Unitas and the legs of Brown. With these highly explosive superstars on the field, offensive fireworks seemed imminent.

Beside having Unitas ringing up points, the Colts also had the best defensive line of the time period. It consisted of hall of famers Art Donovan and Gino Marchetti, plus Don Joyce and 6-6, 284-pound Eugene (Big Daddy) Lipscomb.

Big Daddy was the largest man on the field in the later 1950s, and was murder on opposing teams. He was a devastating run stopper, and with Jim Brown on the menu for the first time against him, Big Daddy was ready to feast. The week prior to this game, Lipscomb was talking to newspaper reporters, and anyone else who would listen, and said that he could hardly wait to get his hands on Brown. It wasn't that Lipscomb had any animosity toward Brown, it was just his way of firing himself up for the big game against Cleveland. It also made for good copy.

With Big Daddy drooling at the possibilities of burying Jim Brown in the turf time after time, the task of containing Lipscomb fell on fourth-year tackle, Jim Ray Smith. Without the Cleveland coaches knowing, Jim Brown and his offensive linemen, Smith in particular, worked out a blocking scheme that they felt could neutralize Baltimore's famed line. It allowed the Baltimore linemen to move the man facing them in any direction they wanted. The Cleveland linemen would then hold them off as long as they could while Jim Brown looked for an opening instead of running to an assigned area. This would allow Brown the freedom to pick and choose where to run. It would also confuse Baltimore on each of Brown's carries.

A soldout Memorial Stadium saw the Browns draw first blood with a Groza field goal. Steve Myhra added a field goal of his own to tie the score at the end of the first quarter. Baltimore missed a golden opportunity to take the lead in the opening quarter after Carl Taseff returned an interception back to the Cleveland 16. Myhra tried another field goal, but the kick went wide.

All the hype surrounding a Brown vs. Unitas scoringfest seemed to be just that, as neither player made a significant move in the first quarter.

Jim Brown changed all that on the third play of the second quarter. Proving that all the hype was true, he took a pitchout from Milt Plum on third-and-ten from the Cleveland 30. The running play completely caught Baltimore off guard, because they were looking for a pass in this situation. Brown shocked them even more by shaking off a lineman, then taking off at full throttle down the sideline. Safetyman Ray Brown tried to stop Brown at the Baltimore 40, but was run over by the fullback in the process.

Bobby Mitchell laid waste to the last defender in Brown's way with a great block, and the fullback was home free to complete the 70-yard touchdown run. Groza capped off Brown's longest run of the season with the conversion to give Cleveland a 10-3 lead.

Not to be overshadowed by Jim Brown in his own stadium, Unitas and his arm took the Colts downfield for a score following the ensuing kickoff. Unitas completed four passes in the drive, with the biggest being a 40-yarder to Jim Mutscheller. Lenny Moore finished the drive off by taking a Unitas pass on fourth down the final six yards. Myhra added the tying extra point.

Jim Ray Smith

Cleveland quickly got into Baltimore territory on their next possession. Thanks to a poor kickoff and a roughing the passer penalty, the Browns had the ball on the Baltimore 32. Mitchell carried for 15, then Brown went the final 17 yards to put Cleveland in front to stay.

Unitas came close to tying the game up near the end of the first half, but on fourth-and-ten from the Cleveland 16, his pass intended for Moore was intercepted by cornerback Bernie Parrish.

Taking advantage of a Junior Wren interception early in the third quarter, Cleveland scored on a 3-yard run by Brown to make the score 24-10 after Groza's conversion.

The Colts came back quickly. From his own 19, Unitas threw a 10-yard sideline pass to Moore, who at first appeared to be neutralized by Parrish. Moore escaped from Parrish with a beautiful move and ran for 71 yards before being stopped on the Cleveland 10. Two plays later, Unitas threw for a touchdown from eight yards out to Jerry Richardson. Myhra's extra point then closed the gap to seven points.

The offensive show continued when Cleveland took the ball 80 yards in 12 plays on their next possession. With his offensive line controlling the Baltimore front four so well, Jim Brown was running at will over and around the Colts. Of all the Cleveland linemen, Jim Ray Smith in particular was giving a yeoman's effort on Big Daddy Lipscomb. Poor Big Daddy wanted to get his hands on Brown so bad, but throughout the game, thanks to Smith, he couldn't even lay a finger on him. With excellent blocking, Brown helped himself to the Baltimore end zone for the fourth time in the game, this time

going in from the 1. Groza's conversion made it 31-17 at the end of three quarters.

Both offenses cooled off for a short time, but at the nine-minute mark of the fourth quarter, things were once again hot. The defending champions refused to die in this one, and closed the gap to seven points after Unitas found his favorite receiver, Raymond Berry, for a 10-yard touchdown.

Despite their will to win, the Colts were laid to rest at the 1:32 mark when Brown capped off a 74-yard drive with his fifth touchdown run of the day. His 1-yard run, and Groza's conversion, made the score 38-24.

Aided by four penalties, the Colts got downfield quickly. Unitas then hit Mutscheller for a touchdown to make it a 38-31 final.

The Jim Brown vs. Johnny Unitas duel definitely lived up to its hype. Brown had his best rushing day of the season, running for 178 yards on 32 carries and five touchdowns. Unitas played like the champion he was by completing 23 of 41 passes for 397 yards and four touchdowns.

After this game, Brown was way out in front of his fellow runners with 737 yards. He never looked back either, and ended the season with 1,329 yards to capture his third straight rushing title. Unfortunately, the Cleveland Browns lost three straight late in the year to finish at 7-5, and a distant second to the 10-2 New York Giants.

The Colts on the other hand, rebounded quite nicely from this defeat. They only lost one more game, and finished at 9-3. They beat the Giants, 31-16, in the NFL title game to repeat as champions.

JIM BROWN TIES HIS SINGLE-GAME RUSHING RECORD

[NOVEMBER 19, 1961]

After recording his fourth straight rushing title in 1960 with 1,257 yards, Jim Brown was once again ahead of the pack when Cleveland met the Philadelphia Eagles on November 19, 1961 at Municipal Stadium. Going into this game, Brown had 853 yards on the ground through nine weeks for the 6-3 Browns.

The Eagles came into town as defending NFL champions, and were tied with New York at 7-2 for first place in the Eastern Conference.

Nine minutes into the game, Philadelphia went up, 3-0, on a 34-yard Bobby Walston field goal. Following the kickoff, Cleveland moved from their 21 to the Philadelphia 16 with Jim Brown carrying five times on the drive. They were unable to capitalize on this drive, but moved to the Eagles' 21 on their next possession as time ran out in the first quarter. The big play of that drive came when Milt Plum threw a screen pass to Jim Brown, and behind great downfield blocking, the fullback powered his way 39 yards.

After an incomplete pass on the first play of the second quarter, Brown ran hard off the left side for 18 yards, then put Cleveland in front, 7-3, with a touchdown run from the 2.

Philadelphia came right back to reclaim the lead with a 12-play, 68-yard touchdown drive to go up, 10-7.

Shortly before the first half ended, Cleveland went 83 yards, and Brown carried most of the load. He caught a pass for 12 yards, and ran five times for 40 more, with the final carry going for a touchdown from three yards out to give the Browns a 14-10 halftime lead. On this scoring run, the Eagles had the line stacked in anticipation of a run up the middle. Once Brown took the handoff and noticed what awaited him if he ran up the gut, he glided along the line, found an opening around the end, and scored with ease.

The rest of this game was all Cleveland, as they scored six straight times in the second half. Jim Brown got the new half going by returning the kickoff 24 yards to the Cleveland 27. Brown didn't normally return kickoffs, but an injury to Preston Powell forced him into service. With Cleveland mixing up the run and pass successfully, it only took them eight plays to go out in front, 21-10. Brown carried for 13 yards on the drive, and when not running, he provided excellent blocking out of the backfield. From the Eagles' 28, Plum went to the pass, and found Bobby Mitchell for the touchdown.

Late in the third quarter, Cleveland regained possession, and looked to eat up as much time off the clock as possible. Up to this time, Paul Brown had called a

brilliant game from the sideline. He opened up the Philadelphia defense by passing quite a bit in the first half. Once the Eagles were sucked in by the pass, Brown mixed things up with running plays, mostly to Jim Brown, and with successful results. Paul Brown now looked to his fullback to be the main offensive weapon for the rest of the afternoon. By halftime, Jim Brown was a bit tired, but got a second wind throughout the third quarter, and was ready to churn out the yardage.

Alternating his runs between right and left tackle, Brown got Cleveland across midfield by running over and around anyone in a Philadelphia uniform. With his blocking being the best it was all season long, Brown was getting stronger while the Eagles were getting tired. Once past the 50-yard line, Brown continued to attack the weary defense. He was virtually unstoppable, carrying the ball four times for 30 yards, and getting the Browns into position for Lou Groza to boot a 22-yard field goal to give Cleveland a 24-10 lead after three quarters.

Jim Brown continued to move the chains as the fourth quarter began. His runs on this day were not long, just effective and time consuming. The Eagles were now beaten dogs, and if they were not convinced just yet, Brown made them believers by upping the Cleveland advantage to 31-10 with a 3-yard touchdown run.

Jimmy Brown

N.F.L. Rushing Leader
5 Consecutive Seasons

Yr.	Att.	Yds.	Ave.
1957	202	942	4.7
1958	257	1527*	5.9
1959	290	1329	4.6
1960	215	1257	5.8
1961	305*	1408	4.6
Totals	1269	6463	5.1

*N.F.L. Record

Drawing by Jim Ponter, of The Bulletin

Jim Brown

The next time Cleveland had the ball, Brown went up the middle for 16. After a gain of four more, Brown got a chance to rest on the next play while Mitchell took the ball 11 yards. It was back to Brown, and he gained 19 yards on the next two carries. Three plays later, Brown ran wide around the right side from the 8-yard line to score his fourth touchdown of the game, and it gave Cleveland a 38-17 lead.

The Eagles managed to make it 38-24 following Brown's fourth touchdown, but went right back to trailing by 21 points after the ensuing kickoff. Mitchell received the kick on his 9-yard line, and with a key block coming from Brown, found himself electrifying the home crowd with a 91-yard return to close out the scoring at 45-24.

At the two-minute warning, Jim Brown was still in the game, and still effective. On his final three carries, he ran for a total of 19 yards to give him 242 yards on the day and a new single-game rushing record. It was later learned, however, that the statisticians had made a mistake and awarded Brown five extra yards. With the five subtracted, it gave Brown 237 yards on 34 carries, which tied his mark set against Los Angeles in 1957. The record would last until O.J. Simpson broke it in 1973.

The win gave Cleveland a share of second place, but they never got close to first place in the conference race. Going 1-2-1 the rest of the way, the Browns finished at 8-5-1 for third place behind New York (10-3-1), and Philadelphia (10-4).

Coming as no surprise, Jim Brown blew past all the other runners to win the NFL's rushing title for an unprecedented fifth straight season with 1,408 yards.

Lou "The Toe" Groza

JIM BROWN SETS NEW SINGLE-SEASON RUSHING RECORD

[1963]

Jim Brown lost out on his bid for a sixth consecutive rushing title in 1962. It proved to be Jim Taylor's year, as the power runner from Green Bay amassed 1,474 yards, to finish 300 yards ahead of his nearest competitor. Brown finished in an unlikely fourth place with 996 yards.

After the 1962 season, which saw the Browns finish 7-6-1 for their worst season in six years, Jim Brown and many other key players were unhappy playing for Paul Brown.

Over the course of his coaching career, Paul Brown ran a tight ship where he was the only one in charge. He called all the plays, and refused to listen to his players' suggestions about what might or might not work. Self-expression or calling audibles were out of the question, even if a change of play could produce something positive. It was looked at by Brown as a form of mutiny, and could cause much grief for the player who stood up to him.

When he took over as coach in 1946, the athlete of the time was used to strict rules, because most of them had just come back from serving in the military during World War II. They felt that playing football professionally was a chance to make a good living, and were willing to pay the price for the opportunity in a time right after the war when jobs were scarce. Whatever Paul Brown said at that time went, and while the team was winning year after year, nobody seemed to mind the tight reins.

It wasn't that the Cleveland players of the later 50s and early 60s didn't have the same passion for the game as those in the 40s. If anything, they maybe had more passion, because they wanted to express their ideas, which in turn could help the team win. Under Paul Brown, however, that was not to be, and eventually time and stubbornness caught up to him as the 1960s came along, and the coach that everyone wanted to be soon became predictable. Other coaches around the league learned from him, and progressed to the point that they were able to beat the master. Unwilling to bend or change his philosophy, Paul

Brown's teams seemed to be on a downward spiral with no way back up. He still produced winning records, but just barely.

This is not to say that Paul Brown's coaching methods were bad. He was a true gentleman who carried himself with a great deal of class throughout his career and life away from the field. Many successful coaches before and after him ran tight regimens which produced championship caliber teams. As stated earlier though, winning championships has a way of making all the bad things seem all right, but take away the success, and smiles quickly turn upside down.

This was the case in late 1962, as Jim Brown and many other players began to get more and more vocal about their feelings toward their coach.

In 1961, 35-year old New York native Art Modell took over ownership of the Cleveland Browns, and unlike previous team owners, Mickey McBride and Dave Jones, he was a hands on executive. He didn't have other outside interests like McBride and Jones, and the Browns were his only means of income at that time. He invested a great deal of his money and others to buy the team, and like all business owners, he wanted to be successful. He also wanted to know about all the facets of the Browns, and that included what went on the field.

In the past, Paul Brown never had to deal with owner involvement. The owners were there to pay the bills. Brown was there to lead the team on the field, and not to be told how to do his job. It seemed pretty cut and dry to Brown, but not to Modell. He wanted to know everything, and that started to get on Brown's nerves. Slowly, throughout the 1961 season, both men started to grow weary of each other. Brown was never second guessed by an owner before, and suddenly he was, which didn't make for too much joyous conversation in the Browns' executive offices.

By 1962, the lid was ready to blow off the pressure cooker that was the Brown-Modell relationship. After seeing another season of average football, coupled with his players dissatisfaction, Modell knew that there was only one way out of this situation.

On January 9, 1963, Modell fired Paul Brown, and replaced him with backfield coach Blanton Collier, who returned to the Browns in 1962 after coaching at the University of Kentucky for eight seasons.

Art Modell

Collier had spent nine total seasons as Brown's assistant, but their coaching styles were completely different. Like Brown, Collier was one of the best teachers in the game, with offensive football being his specialty, but unlike Brown, Collier was open to suggestions by the players. He was a kind man who was open for ideas on how to improve. He became more of a father figure to the team, but just like a parent, he could be stern when the situation called for it. Of all the head coaches in Cleveland Browns history, Collier went down as the most beloved by his players. He also was a winner. He was the type of coach that you wanted to play and win for. With a new sense of purpose, the Cleveland Browns looked to the 1963 season as a rebirth, especially Jim Brown, who was about to rewrite the record books again.

The Blanton Collier years began on a beautiful September 15 afternoon in Cleveland, as did Jim Brown's run for the record. Like anyone starting a new job,

Blanton Collier

Collier was nervous before the game. What made it even tougher was taking over for a legend, but Jim Brown and the rest of the team made Collier's nerves settle down quickly by beating Washington, 37-14.

The Browns rolled up 543 yards on offense, and Jim Brown ran for 162 yards on 15 carries and scored two touchdowns. He also caught three passes for 100 yards and a touchdown. Early in the second quarter with Cleveland up, 10-7, Frank Ryan threw a screen pass to Brown from his own 17. Behind solid blocking, Brown got up some speed, ran into and over some defenders at midfield, then outraced everyone to the end zone to complete the 83-yard catch and run. The next time Cleveland had possession, they went 52 yards for another touchdown with a well-balanced attack. Brown capped the drive off with a 10-yard run to give Cleveland a 24-7 halftime lead. Brown's final touchdown of the day came after taking a pitchout on his own 20. With tackle John Brown throwing the key block that sprung him, Jim Brown sprinted through the secondary without much interference.

The new regime of Blanton Collier's got underway in impressive fashion. Everything clicked on offense, especially the blocking. Before the regular season began, the offensive line was hit with nagging injuries. They also lost two key members of the line when Mike McCormack retired, and Jim Ray Smith was traded to Dallas. Nobody would have ever known there was anything wrong with them on this day, however, because they played brilliantly on both run blocking and pass protection.

Pride. That one word seemed to be tattooed on Cleveland's offensive line after seeing their work unleash the greatness that was Jim Brown in 100-degree heat the following week in a 41-24 win in Dallas. Behind incredible blocking, Brown came away from the Texas inferno with 232 yards rushing on just 20 carries, and scored on two long runs. The first one came in the second quarter. From his 39-yard line, Brown ran off tackle, and seemed to be stopped after a gain of three. The defense then eased up when they thought Brown was stopped. He managed to break free much to the surprise of the defense, and outran the secondary for a 71-yard touchdown. Brown's other touchdown run came with 2:17 left in the game after he shot through the middle and went untouched from 62 yards out. Cleveland never got the ball back for Brown to make a run at a new single-game record. After the first two games, Jim Brown was already way out in front of all other runners with 394 yards.

After being overshadowed for two weeks, it was the defense that stole the headlines in a 20-6 win at home over Los Angeles. On an ugly, rainy day, the offense was slowed up in the mud, but not Jim Brown, who seemed to be like the U.S. Postal Service, by delivering no matter what the weather conditions were like. He had 95 yards on 22 carries and two more touchdowns. On of his scores came after defensive end Paul Wiggin recovered a fumble deep in Los Angeles territory with the Browns trailing for the first time in the young season, 3-0. Brown then put Cleveland on top to stay by running around the left end from 17 yards out. Besides Wiggin's fumble recovery, the defense held the Rams to just two field goals, and came up with an impressive goal line stand in the third quarter to preserve the win.

Frank Ryan

The Pittsburgh Steelers came to town next sporting a 2-0-1 record and one of the toughest defensive lines in the league. In front of a record crowd numbering 84,684, the Browns came back four times to win, 35-23. Jim Brown did the most damage, as he attacked the heart of the Pittsburgh defense with power runs right at the linemen. He scored the first Cleveland touchdown from the 8, and set up another one with a 49-yard gain in the third quarter. He then threw the key block which sprung Frank Ryan for a touchdown to finish the drive off. Brown ended the game with 23 carries for 175 yards.

Fans numbering over 5,000 turned out at Cleveland Hopkins Airport to greet the Browns after they beat hated rival New York, 35-24, to remain undefeated. It was a ritual on the Browns to go out and see a movie the night before a game. Prior to this game against the Giants, the team saw

"The Running Man". On a beautiful afternoon the following day in Yankee Stadium, both teams saw the sequel, but Cleveland enjoyed it more.

Jim Brown was the running man long before Hollywood made the film of the same title, and he proved it by pounding his way for 123, tough, painful yards. The Giants keyed on him all day, hitting him extra hard, especially middle linebacker Sam Huff, who was regarded as one of the hardest tacklers of his time. Brown's running also accounted for three touchdowns, which was the first time in his career that he scored more than one in a game against New York. His first one tied the game at 7-7 when he smashed right into the middle of the New York line from the 1 to finish a 79-yard drive. Brown really came to life in the second half with Cleveland trailing 17-14. After taking a handoff, he slid to his left and went around the end. Instantly, he saw blockers and open field in front of him. At first he was caught behind the line of scrimmage, but the hold on him wasn't strong enough, and he broke away. After this slight delay, Brown ran straight down the sideline untouched to record a 32-yard touchdown run. His other touchdown came in the third quarter on a 72-yard reception. With five games under his belt, Jim Brown had 797 yards on the ground, and no one near him in the race to the rushing title.

Cleveland registered its longest opening win streak since 1953 with its most lopsided victory of the season, a 37-7 thrashing of the Philadelphia Eagles. Still banged up from the beating he took in New York, Jim Brown showed no signs of wear and tear by making his way through the Eagles for 144 yards rushing.

At the end of this game, Brown had 8,390 career rushing yards, surpassing Joe Perry as the NFL's all-time leading ground gainer. Perry was still active, but in his 14th season, and not much of a force to regain the top spot. For the first time in the '63 season, Brown didn't register a rushing touchdown, but did find his way to the end zone with a 10-yard pass from Frank Ryan. The Browns completely dominated the Eagles, 500 yards to just 161, and were now up in the Eastern Conference race by two full games over New York and St. Louis.

All good things must end, and Collier saw his spotless coaching record end in ugly fashion in front of a standing-room-only crowd of 84,213 Clevelanders. Things started bad when Jim Brown fumbled on the second play of the game, and then escalated until the Giants rolled to a 33-6 victory. An inspired New York defense led by Sam Huff clamped down on the NFL's number-one offense, and Jim Brown especially, limiting him to only 40 yards on nine carries. The win put the Browns at 6-1, and cut their conference lead to one game at the halfway mark of the season.

Brown and the rest of his teammates rebounded from the New York massacre with a 23-17 win in Philadelphia. After the opening kickoff, Brown ran around right end for eight yards, and added four more up the middle on the next play. Two plays later, from the Cleveland 38, Brown swept the right side with blockers in front of him. With tight end John Brewer wiping out a safetyman, Brown had no opposition on his way to a 62-yard touchdown run, which was his first on the ground in three weeks. Taking advantage of a defense racked with injuries, Brown carried 28 times for 223 yards, to give him 1,194 yards on the season.

For the third straight week, the Cleveland passing game had sputtered, and all the Steelers had to do in their rematch was key on Jim Brown, which they did in a 9-7 win. Brown still managed to gain 99 yards, and helped Cleveland get their only score by running for 45 yards in a drive that led to a Ryan-to-Gary Collins 11-yard touchdown pass. The Steelers won the game by pinning Cleveland deep at their own 3-yard line, and then tackling Brown in the end zone for a safety.

For the first time in 1963, the Browns fell out of first place by dropping their third game in four weeks to St. Louis, 20-14. Things started out good, as Jim Brown swept to the outside behind good blocking, and ran for a 59-yard touchdown on Cleveland's second offensive play of the game. He finished the day with 154 yards on 22 carries.

Brown's next performance was way below his average, as Dallas held him to a season-low 51 yards on 17 carries, but Cleveland won, 27-17, to once again own a piece of first place with New York and St. Louis. The offense was still not in sync, and the Browns were helped by four interceptions, one of which was returned for a touchdown.

Jim Brown only needed 29 yards to break his 1958 season rushing record, and it didn't take him long to do in a rematch with the Cardinals. Getting revenge for their loss two weeks earlier, the Browns beat St. Louis 24-10 on the road to stay in first place. They got their ninth win of the year thanks to a well-balanced attack, which was lacking for six weeks. Brown took care of the ground work by running for 179 yards and two touchdowns, to

give him a new single-season rushing record of 1,677 for the time being.

Brown added 61 yards to his new rushing record in week thirteen, but it didn't seem to matter as Cleveland suffered their worst defeat of the season, a 38-10 loss to the Detroit Lions. Up to this time, the Browns never beat the Lions in a regular season game, and this one hurt the most because it eliminated them from the Eastern Conference race. The Browns fell behind early, and became predictable by throwing most of the time. This took away the running of Jim Brown, who only carried 13 times.

Despite another miss at the championship game, the Browns finished the 1963 season on a high note with a 27-20 win in Washington, which gave them a 10-4 record, and the most wins in a season since 1953. Jim Brown ended his record-setting season against the same team he began it against. His 125 yards against the Redskins gave him a season total of 1,863 rushing yards, which at the time seemed to be unbeatable. O.J. Simpson proved that the record was beatable by breaking it in 1973 with 2,003 yards. At the end of the season, Jim Brown received every possible award that a runner could get, including the NFL Most Valuable Player Award, which he shared with New York quarterback Y.A. Tittle, who led the Giants to a third straight Eastern Conference title.

Jim Brown was never one to dwell on records. All he wanted was to be a member of a championship team, and all his efforts were geared toward that one elusive prize which always seemed to slip out of his reach. In his next season, however, Jim Brown and the Cleveland Browns would grab on to the then-elusive prize and hold on with a tighter grip.

CLEVELAND BEATS NEW YORK TO WIN 1964 EASTERN CONFERENCE TITLE

[DECEMBER 12, 1964]

Going into week thirteen of the 1964 season, the Browns were leading the Eastern Conference by a game-and-a-half with a 9-2-1 record, and a win over the second place St. Louis Cardinals would give them their first conference title in seven years. The Browns were very confident when they traveled to St. Louis to play what they felt would be a title-clinching game. They were so confident in fact that there were four cases of champagne ready to be brought into the locker room once it looked like victory was assured.

On a cold December 5 in St. Louis, the Browns jumped out to an early 3-0 lead, and thought it wouldn't be long until the sweet taste of champagne was hitting their taste buds. The only problem with the rest of this game was the fact that nobody told the Cardinals to lie down and die. Up to this time, the Cardinals had not won, or even come close to winning, any type of championship in 16 years. They were just as hungry as the Browns for a chance to play for an NFL championship, not to mention the fact that they were a very good football team in the mid-sixties. The Cardinals came to life after spotting the Browns those three points, and won going away, 28-19. They chipped away at the Cleveland defense with short passes, and tormented Frank Ryan with blitzes all day. They also chipped away at the Browns' lead in the conference, which went down to half-a-game going into the season finale with longtime nemesis New York.

Between 1956 and 1963, the New York Giants were the toast of the Eastern Conference, winning it six out of those eight seasons. By 1964, however, age finally caught up to the once-feared New Yorkers, and they were about to close out one of their worst seasons in franchise history. Despite being 2-9-2 going into the game with Cleveland, the Giants were still capable of winning, and would have loved nothing more than to spoil the Browns' chances at a trip to the championship game.

The doubters were out in full force as the Browns geared up for their important season finale in New York. They saw Cleveland come this far before, only to lose out to the Giants when it counted most. They also questioned Frank Ryan's ability at quarterback.

During his two seasons as Cleveland's starting signal caller, the 28-year-old Ryan was considered erratic at times. In 1963, he started the season off very well, but ended it on a poor note. His misfortunes continued into the '64 campaign, and after a few games, there was talk of benching him in favor of backup Jim Ninowski.

Blanton Collier decided to stick with Ryan, and with him at the controls, the Browns saw themselves one game away from a title. Ryan didn't let Collier down, and worked hard at practice throughout the season to hone his skills. He was more often than not the last player off the field after practice each and every day.

On a gloomy, damp Saturday afternoon in Yankee Stadium, the Browns took the field with hopes of erasing any doubt that they were a championship-caliber team. The only obstacle in their way was the New York Giants.

Shortly after 2:00 pm on that dismal Saturday afternoon, Lou Groza kicked off to begin the Browns' quest at becoming the new Eastern Conference champions.

Veteran quarterback Y.A. Tittle, who retired after this game, began his 176th pro game by handing off two straight times. Unable to get a ground game going early, Tittle had the same problem through the air, as Joe Morrison dropped his third down pass.

After receiving the punt on fourth down, Cleveland advanced deep enough for Groza to put the Browns on top, 3-0, with a 39-yard field goal. That was the

way the first quarter ended, as neither team could establish any foothold on the other.

The 37-year-old Tittle looked good early in the second quarter when he directed the Giants on a superb 76-yard drive. With pinpoint passing and the help of a 15-yard penalty, Tittle got New York a 7-3 lead on a 7-yard touchdown pass to Dick James.

With the Giants' masterful scoring drive, the doubters were sure to be thinking, "Here we go again. Another season of being a bridesmaid but never a bride". Maybe there were other colorful expressions used to describe what people were feeling, but this one might have been one of the cleanest.

It became apparent on Cleveland's next drive that they were also tired of being a bridesmaid, and set out to be the bride after seven long years. It took the Browns only nine plays to regain the lead. After seven running plays, Frank Ryan looked to pass from the New York 12. As he faded into the pocket, his protection broke down, and he was forced to tuck the ball under his arm and make a run for it. When he was closing in on the goal line, Ryan was hit, and after falling to the ground, fumbled the ball. The Giants recovered for what they thought was a legitimate fumble, but one of the officials was right there to signal a Cleveland touchdown. The official ruled that Ryan had crossed the goal line before fumbling, which meant that the play was dead, and the touchdown counted. Groza added the conversion, and Cleveland was in front to stay, 10-7.

Six plays after Ryan's touchdown, Tittle threw a pass intended for Frank Gifford on the Cleveland 40. It was at that moment that Bernie Parrish came up with a key interception to stop New York's momentum. Parrish waited until Tittle released the ball, then came up on Gifford at full speed. It was a gamble, because if he missed the ball, Gifford could have caught it and possibly gone for a score that might have changed the complexion of the game. Parrish's gamble paid off, as he picked the ball off on the run, and took it to the New York 29 before being blasted out of bounds.

On the fifth play of the drive following Parrish's theft, Ryan found Gary Collins on a slant pattern from the 11-yard line. Collins was well covered on his route, but made the catch in the end zone with a defender hanging on his leg. Groza's extra point made the score 17-7.

With time running out in the first half, Tittle tried to get the Giants back in the game, but another interception killed the drive. This time middle linebacker Vince Costello came up with the interception, and it proved to be the last pass ever thrown by Tittle. In the second half, he watched from the sideline as his heir apparent, rookie Gary Wood, took over.

Costello's interception gave the Browns the ball on the New York 48. With time running out, Ryan called timeout to discuss his options with Blanton Collier. Rookie receiver Paul Warfield had told Ryan that he could beat his man long. Ryan knew that a touchdown at this point could just about put the game on ice, so he told Collier what

he wanted to do. Collier felt that a long pass to Warfield might work, and told his quarterback to call a Double Z Out, which meant that Warfield would first fake to the middle, then cut back to the outside. At the snap, Warfield got such a huge jump on the man covering him that he changed his rout and ran for the goal line. Ryan saw what was happening, and after adjusting to it, threw a high pass to Warfield that went for 47 yards. With 17 seconds

Paul Warfield

left, and the ball on the New York 1, Ryan surprised the Giants by rolling to his right. New York was expecting a run, but by the time they saw Ryan rolling out to pass, it was too late. He threw to Ernie Green for the touchdown, and with Groza's conversion, the Browns went into the intermission in complete control, 24-7.

Instead of resting on their laurels, the Browns continued to attack. They didn't want to get lazy and allow the Giants to get back into the game, and by the end of the third quarter, there wasn't any chance of that happening.

Ryan must have liked throwing that touchdown pass to Ernie Green so much before the half, that he went right back to him at the beginning of the third quarter. After faking to Jim Brown, Ryan dropped back and found Green for a 25-yard scoring pass to give Cleveland a 31-7 lead. The play came off so well thanks in large part to Brown, who faked the handoff so convincingly that the New York defense swarmed him while Green slipped by unnoticed.

Ryan was having so much fun throwing touchdowns in this game, that he decided to keep doing it. Warfield, who caught 5 passes for 103 yards on the day, was Ryan's next recipient of a touchdown pass, with this one coming from 7 yards out to make it 38-7.

Jim Brown had 99 yards rushing, but decided to join in on Ryan's passing clinic. He caught a pass on the New York 5, and after putting a splendid move on a defender, made his way into the end zone with Ryan's fifth touchdown pass of the game.

With fifteen minutes standing in the way of crowning Cleveland with the East-

ern Conference title, Ryan gave way to backup Jim Ninowski with the score 45-7. All the hard work and extra practice that Ryan put in during the season seemed all worthwhile on this day. He left the game with an NFL record 92% completion rating after hitting on 12 of 13 passes. He

Ernie Green (44) and Leroy Kelly (48).

threw for 202 yards, not to mention for five touchdowns, and added another one on the ground. He called his own game, and did a brilliant job mixing up the run and pass to keep New York off balance. Not bad for being criticized as erratic.

Ninowski picked up where Ryan left off. In his brief appearance, Ninowski completed 4 of 6 passes for 73 yards and one touchdown. After the Giants scored on a Gary Wood to Aaron Thomas pass, Ninowski threw to rookie Walter Roberts for a 24-yard touchdown. On the game's final play, Wood and Thomas teamed up again to make the final score 52-20.

The champagne that was ready to be popped in St. Louis was no where to be found in the locker room after the game. Maybe the organization became a bit superstitious after the loss to the Cardinals, and didn't want to take anything for granted. As the Browns were on their way home, however, the bubbly was uncorked up in the plane, and the celebration was under way. At least 7,000 fans came out to the airport to welcome home their conquering heroes, and the revelry lasted well into the night. After a few days of soaking in the fact that they were headed to the NFL championship game, it was back to work time for the Browns. They had two weeks to prepare themselves for the biggest game of their careers, and against one of the toughest teams ever assembled.

Paul Wiggin was a defensive end from 1957-67.

BROWNS WIN 1964 NFL CHAMPIONSHIP

[DECEMBER 27, 1964]

Devastating. This one word from the English language can best be used to sum up the 1964 Baltimore Colts. With a mixture of veterans, many of whom were on their back-to-back championship teams in 1958-59, and young players performing above expectation, the Colts crushed 12 out of their 14 regular-season opponents. They easily won the Western Conference by four games over the 8-5-1 Green Bay Packers and Minnesota Vikings.

After an opening-day loss to Minnesota, the Colts won eleven in a row before losing to Detroit in a game that had no meaning anyway. To say the Colts won eleven in a row would be an understatement. They completely dominated those teams. The Colts rang up a league-high 428 points for the third highest total up to that time in NFL history. Their 4,779 total yards also led the league in 1964.

Quarterback Johnny Unitas was at his peak in 1964, and was regarded as the best at his position. He earned his third all-pro selection by completing 52 percent of his passes for 2,824 yards, 19 touchdowns, and a minuscule six interceptions.

Stealing more headlines than Unitas in 1964 was running back Lenny Moore. After suffering through two seasons of severe injuries, Moore came into training camp with little hope of making the team. Refusing to give up, he worked hard to make the team, and then made headlines. He ran for a team high 584 yards, caught 21 passes for 472 yards, and set a then-NFL record 20 touchdowns to lead the league in scoring with 120 points. Moore's remarkable turnaround earned him an all-pro selection, the Comeback Player of the Year award, and the NFL's Most Valuable Player trophy.

Baltimore also had the league's top receiving corps in Raymond Berry, Johnny Orr, and John Mackey. Berry was Unitas' favorite target, and even after ten seasons, he was still trouble for defensive backfields. Possessing great hands and moves, Berry led the team with 43 catches for 663 yards and 6 touchdowns. Jimmy Orr was Baltimore's deep threat.

With the ability to shake off defenders and haul in long passes, Orr could blow a game wide open with just one catch. Rounding out the receivers was tight end John Mackey, who was a bulldozer-like player who was capable of taking a short pass then running over people for big gains.

Up front the Colts had the best offensive line in football, and four of the five were starters on Baltimore's championship teams in 1958-59. Anchoring the line was guard Jim Parker, who earned his seventh straight all-pro selection. Parker went down in history as one of the top-rated linemen of all time. Left tackle Bob Vogel joined Parker on the first team all-pro squad, while right guard Alex Sandusky and right tackle George Preas made second team all-pro.

On the other side of the ball, Baltimore's defense was just as impressive. Mixing experience and youth, this unit gave up the fewest points (225), and were ranked third in overall defensive play.

At age 37, defensive end Gino Marchetti was still regarded as the most feared pass rusher in the game, and in 1964 he was named all-pro for the eighth straight season. The other end, Ordell Braase, was also an accomplished pass rusher, and tackles Guy Reese and Fred Miller were able to use their strength to overpower opponents and get into the backfield quickly.

The linebacking was rich with experience, and led by blitzing expert Don Shinnick. Rounding out the defense was a fast secondary led by hard hitter Bob Boyd.

The head man on the sideline who was responsible for putting together this incredible team was 34-year old former Browns' player and Cleveland native Don Shula. After seeing his team falter somewhat in the years preceding the back-to-back championships in 1958-59, Baltimore owner Carroll Rosenbloom fired Weeb Ewbank, and replaced him in 1963 with Shula.

Despite winning the Eastern Conference, the 1964 Cleveland Browns were dubbed the "Laugh Champs" by opposing coaches and reporters who felt they were not a dominant team, but just a lucky one that managed to come up with an interception or fumble recovery at the right time to pull out a close game.

Most of the doubt centered around the defense, even though this unit was the one that came up with the interception or fumble recovery to help out in those close games. Despite this, the bottom line was the numbers, and Cleveland's defensive unit as a whole ranked dead last in the NFL. They were regarded as having a slow secondary, a front four that ranked last in sacks, and a linebacking corps that was good, but vulnerable to the run because they had to drop back into pass coverage a great deal of the time to help out the secondary. One positive thing that could be said of this unit was about their toughness inside their own 20.

Another positive element that the defense had was tackle Dick Modzelewski, who came over to Cleveland in a trade with New York prior to the start of the '64 season. He brought with him a will to win from those championship teams in New York, and in no time at all, he passed his desire on to the rest of Browns with a leadership-by-example approach.

Modzelewski quickly took second-year tackle Jim Kanicki under his wing and groomed him into a solid performer.

Jim Kanicki

Kanicki's position was one of the spots that the experts felt would hurt Cleveland's chances going into the title game. Opposing Kanicki would be possibly the greatest offensive lineman of all time in Jim Parker. With Parker facing a youngster with little experience in such a big game, the experts saw Parker pushing Kanicki around all day without much resistance. If that would be the case, the Baltimore running game would flourish over Kanicki's spot for long gains almost at will.

Joining Kanicki and Modzelewski on the line were ends Bill Glass and Paul Wiggin. Even though the front four were last in the league in sacks with 18 1/2, Glass was still thought of as a good pass rusher, and his eight sacks led the team. Wiggin added 7 1/2 sacks, and played his position almost error free.

Regarded as the best group on the Cleveland defense were the linebacking corps of team captain Galen Fiss, Vince Costello, and all-pro Jim Houston.

The worst group of the unit according to football insiders was the secondary of Cleveland native Larry Benz, defensive signal caller Bernie Parrish, Ross Fichtner, Bobby Franklin, and Walter Beach, who was the fastest with a 9.6 clocking in the 100-yard

dash. To compensate for their lack of speed, the secondary played quite a bit of zone coverage throughout the year. Beside Parker's dominance over Kanicki, the secondary was another area in which Baltimore had a huge advantage. With the best quarterback of the era in his prime, the experts saw Unitas ripping Cleveland's defensive backfield to shreds.

Not all the prognosis was bad for the Browns going into this game. At least some credit was given to the offense, and the fact that they had the greatest running back of all time on their side. In 1964, Jim Brown was firmly entrenched as the NFL's

Bill Glass

Bernie Parrish

all-time leading rusher, and finished this season with 1,446 yards to capture his seventh rushing title in eight campaigns, and his seventh spot on the all-pro team.

Brown's running mate was Ernie Green, who was one of the most versatile players of this time. Whatever was asked of him, Green did it well. He ran for 491 yards, caught 25 passes, and had a combined total of 10 touchdowns. He was also one of the top blocking backs in the league.

When talking about great offensive lines through the years, Cleveland's has to be mentioned. If one looks at a picture of Jim Brown running the ball on a sweep, chances are that guard Gene Hickerson or all-pro tackle Dick Schafrath will be shown in the picture leading him around the end. Both of these men should already be in the hall of fame, but hopefully someday their talents will be recognized by the election committee, and they will be forever immortalized along with Jim Brown in Canton, Ohio. Other members of the offensive line were Monte Clark and John Brown, who shared time at the other tackle position, guard John Wooten, and center John Morrow.

The Cleveland receiving department was right up there at the top of the league thanks to Gary Collins, rookie Paul Warfield, and tight end Johnny Brewer. Nicknamed "Mr. Post-Pattern", Collins made that route his trademark by catching 35 passes for 544 yards and eight touchdowns. Cleveland's number-one draft pick in 1964, Warfield used 9.6 speed over 100-yards to catch a team high 52 passes for 920 yards and nine touchdowns on his way to all-pro honors. Usually used as a blocker, Brewer still found the time to gather in 25 passes for three touchdowns.

Gene Hickerson

Responsible for making the Cleveland offense go in 1964 was quarterback Frank Ryan. Considered erratic at times, Ryan proved more often than not that he was an accomplished field general. He had a genius I.Q. , and earned a Doctorate Degree in Mathematics during the off-seasons. On the field, Ryan was dubbed Dr. Cool by his teammates because of his poise. During the season, he used that poise to complete 52 percent of his passes for 2,404 yards, and a league-leading 25 touchdown passes.

Even with all their offensive firepower, the Cleveland Browns were still regarded as laughable chokers who didn't even deserve to be on the same field with the Baltimore Colts. It was said that the worst Western Conference team could beat the best from the Eastern Conference, and that the Browns' only claim to fame on game day would be that of the team who got mauled by the wrecking machine from Baltimore. With all the factors weighed in, the oddsmakers made the Colts 17-point favorites to win, but by kickoff, the odds were brought down to seven points.

On Sunday, December 27, Cleveland Municipal Stadium hosted its fifth NFL championship game, with 79,544 in attendance. Unlike in today's playoffs, in which the teams with the best records have home field advantage, the pre-Super Bowl playoffs alternated hosting the NFL title game each year between the two conferences. Thanks to the luck of the draw, Cleveland got to host the game with a 10-3-1 record as opposed to Baltimore's 12-2 slate.

The field was damp even though it had been covered all week by a tarpaulin. A week prior to the game, groundskeepers tried to dry the field with huge blowers which seemed to help a little. Game day itself was gloomy, as big thick gray clouds hung over the stadium, and temperatures remained near 30 degrees throughout the contest. Making it seem colder

was a 15-mile-per-hour wind that blew in off Lake Erie through the open end of the stadium.

Cleveland won the coin toss and elected to receive, and at 1:45p.m., the 32nd NFL title game got underway between the "Laugh Champs" and the invincible Colts.

Lou Michaels kicked off to Walter Roberts in the end zone, and he brought the ball out to the Cleveland 21 before Neal Petties tackled him.

The Browns usually started a game off with Jim Brown carrying, but Blanton

Gary Collins

Collier and his staff felt that Baltimore might be aware of this through film study. In an attempt to mix the Colts up early, Ryan faked a handoff to Brown and gave the ball to Green. The Colts weren't fooled at all, and Marchetti knocked Green down after a gain of two. Brown got his first call on the next play, and shot through the line for eight yards and a first down on the 31.

After Green and Brown each carried for a total of four yards, the Browns were penalized for taking too much time, and faced a third-and-eighteen situation. Dropping back to pass for the first time against the fierce Baltimore pass rush, Ryan found the going easy, and got off a screen pass to Brown on the 24. The big fullback then gathered up a good head of steam and made his way 23 yards upfield until two defenders teamed up to bring him down near midfield. In their first five plays, the Browns made it look easy against the Colts, and were moving. Unfortunately, the Colts woke up and stopped them on third-and-six.

Collins doubled as the punter, and kicked away on fourth down. Following a holding penalty against the Browns, the Colts got their first crack at the weak Cleveland defense. On first down from the Baltimore 28, Lenny Moore made the experts look good by running off right tackle for an easy 15-yard gain.

On the next play, Orr took off

Jim Houston

looking to go deep with Cleveland in man-for-man coverage. Parrish stayed right with him, and forced him to break sooner than he wanted to. Linebacker Jim Houston helped out by dropping back into the passing lane in an attempt to block Unitas' view. With his main receiver so well covered, and his protection breaking down, Unitas was forced to run. Galen Fiss made first contact to slow him up, then Ross Fichtner and Jim Kanicki finished him off after a gain of seven. Even though Unitas had run for a good gain, the supposedly weak Cleveland defense had passed its first test against the famed passing arm of Unitas by not allowing him the opportunity to throw. They felt that

Unitas could hurt them less with his legs than with his golden arm.

The Browns got another lift on the next play when fullback Jerry Hill fumbled at midfield and Modzelewski recovered. Chalk one up for the "Laugh Champs", who once again were saved by a turnover.

Jim Brown ran for seven yards on first down to give Cleveland their deepest penetration at the Baltimore 44. Two plays later Brown picked up another first down with a gain of three. After Brown and Green netted only five yards on the next two plays, Ryan chucked the conservative game plan, and looked to attack the Colts with a long pass. Behind good protection, Ryan had time to spot Warfield inside the Baltimore 20. With the pass closing in on Warfield's hands, the rookie receiver slipped on the slick field and fell. Linebacker Don Shinnick managed to keep his footing, however, and intercepted on the 10. He got to his 24 before being stopped.

After three running plays got the Colts a first down on their 33, Unitas called for a pass to Berry. Walter Beach was in man-for-man coverage with Berry, and stayed right with him as he cut to the left sideline. Beach suffered the same fate as Warfield when he lost his footing at the most inopportune time. Thanks to the slippery field, Berry caught the ball for a 23-yard gain at

the Cleveland 41. The first quarter ended with the Colts on the move at the Cleveland 24.

The second quarter began with the Browns determined to stop Baltimore's momentum. They turned up the pass rush, the linebackers dropped back to plug up the passing lanes, and the secondary managed to stay with the receivers. It seemed that everything Cleveland did wrong on defense during the season was

Galen Fiss

suddenly working out right. Because of this tremendous effort, Unitas was flushed out of the pocket, and could only find Mackey for a gain of two yards on third down.

With their drive stalled at the Cleveland 19, the Colts brought in their field goal unit on fourth down. It looked like an easy chip shot for kicker Lou Michaels, but the snap to holder Bob Boyd came at him too high. He tried to run for a first down, but an alert Vince Costello caught Boyd right away, and slammed him down for a nine-yard loss.

Taking over on their own 28, the Browns ran the ball eight straight times to get to the Baltimore 39. On first down from there, Ryan missed with a pass, and the Browns returned to the ground game. Brown tore through the defense for ten yards, but an illegal procedure penalty knocked Cleveland back to the Baltimore 40. A sack by Marchetti and Braase on Ryan pushed them nine more yards back. What looked so promising for the Browns a few plays earlier ended with Collins punting on fourth-and-eighteen.

With time running out in the first half, the Colts took over on their 20. On second-and-four, Unitas faked to Hill, then took a short drop into the pocket. Almost immediately, Modzelewski got past center Dick Szymanski, and was coming in hard on Unitas. Joining Modzelewski from the right side was Bill Glass. Realizing that he was about to get sacked, Unitas flipped a screen pass to Moore out of the backfield. With Parker and Szymanski out in front of him, Moore was gaining speed, and looked like he could go all the way for a touchdown. Thanks to captain Galen Fiss coming up with the biggest defensive play of the game, he

didn't. Fiss crashed through Parker and Szymanski to dump Moore in the backfield for a loss of five yards.

Unitas got the lost yardage back plus nine more yards with a completion to Berry. After Moore gained six yards on two plays, Unitas connected with Orr at midfield.

Up to this time, Unitas was perfect, hitting on five of five attempts despite constant pressure from the Cleveland front four. With the two-minute warning coming up, Unitas wanted to at least get his team close enough for a field goal attempt before time ran out in the half.

Just like time after time throughout the half, Unitas had pressure coming at him as he dropped back to pass. Once again seeing a wave of white jerseys coming at him, Unitas rushed a long pass to Mackey. The ball hit Mackey on the thigh, and bounced into the air at the Cleveland 30. Both Costello and Fiss were in the area, and it was Costello who grabbed the ball out of the air on the 29. He was quickly brought down by Orr before he could get going. The officials gave the two-minute warning, and the "Laugh Champs" once again dodged another bullet.

Ryan went to the air on first down, but his pass was batted down by Marchetti. Two plays later, he was luckier, and connected with Collins at midfield. An incomplete pass and two penalties followed, and Collins punted on fourth-and-twenty-two. His kick went for a whopping 58 yards, and Jerry Logan called for it on the Baltimore 29. Three plays later, the first half ended with Unitas throwing an incomplete pass intended for Berry. This marked only the second time in title game history that the first half

Dick Modzelewski

ended in a scoreless tie.

Even though the game was scoreless, Cleveland felt that they had a slight edge because of their ability to play on an even keel with a team that was supposed to come into town and eat them alive. By all accounts, this game should have been out of reach for Cleveland by the half.

Much of the thanks had to go to Blanton Collier, his staff, and defensive signal caller Bernie Parrish, in getting the Browns into the locker room dead even.

Collier was one of the best coaches at getting his team ready for one specific game. He achieved this with intense film study, and after watching countless hours of game film, he knew the opposition better than they knew themselves. In the final analysis, Collier called for his team to heat up the pass rush, and seal off the passing lanes, which seemed pretty basic for most defensive game plans. It was the execution that mattered, and after much practice and film study, the Browns were executing their game plan to perfection.

Parrish also studied film of the Baltimore offense for close to 100 hours looking for any possible edge. In his search Parrish noticed that Baltimore's right cornerback, Len Lyles, lined up nose to nose with the receiver he was covering. At the snap, Lyles would bump his man with a quick thrust to throw off his timing. This method of play is called bump and run. After seeing Lyles do this on film time after time, Parrish had a revelation. During a Baltimore practice session, Lyles lined up opposite Raymond Berry, and for him to impress the coaches, Lyles must have used this technique on Berry to secure a starting job. Parrish relayed this information to Walter Beach, who in turn used Lyles' technique on Berry, and did a great job containing him throughout the first half.

Parrish also noticed that defensive backs who went up against the Colts had a tendency to play a few yards back off the line of scrimmage. This helped give them less ground to make up after the receivers broke off the line. Baltimore's receivers became so used to this that they expected it to happen all the time. This technique worked to Baltimore's advantage because it gave them more room to go deep.

Parrish and his defensive teammates then worked out a strategy based on all the informa-

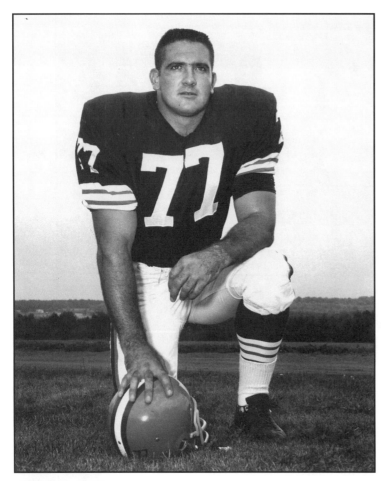

Dick Schafrath

tion gathered through film studies. They felt that if they moved up closer to their man at the line of scrimmage, it might cause the receivers to break quicker than they wanted to, which would help to throw off Unitas' timing. The linebackers would then drop deeper than usual into pass coverage to clog up the passing lanes, and with the pass rush taunting Unitas, anything was possible.

The Cleveland defense managed to follow their assignments to perfection throughout the first half, and were able to shut down the famed Baltimore attack. The big question as the second half got underway was if the Browns could continue to execute the same way for another thirty minutes.

Lou Groza got the second half going with a great kickoff that sailed deep into the end zone for no return.

Cleveland's defense looked like they lost no momentum during the intermission, and they made easy work of the Colts on their opening drive. On fourth down, Tom Gilburg, punting into a strong wind, shanked the ball off the side of his foot. With the wind holding the ball up, it dropped out of bounds at the Baltimore 48 after going 25 yards.

Thanks to Gilburg's poor punt, the Browns began their first series of the second half with excellent field position. Brown carried on the opening play, but was sacked behind the line of scrimmage for a loss of five yards. Brown made up for the loss on the following play after taking a Ryan screen pass in the left flat. Behind solid blocking from Wooten and Schafrath, he made his way 15 yards before three defenders dragged him down at the Baltimore 37. Unable to move but one yard closer on the next three downs,

the Browns called on Groza to attempt a 43-yard field goal. With the help of a 30-mile-per-hour wind, the ball split the uprights to give the underdog Browns a 3-0 lead.

Groza got off another monstrous blast on the ensuing kickoff, and once again there was no return attempted. Unitas started off this drive with an incomplete pass, and dropped back once more on second down, but was sacked by Jim Kanicki for a loss of two. Kanicki was supposed to be one of the weak spots for the Browns, but he was playing the best game of his young career against the great Jim Parker, the man who was predicted to pound him into submission. After the sack, Unitas completed a pass to Tony Lorick for five yards, but it wasn't enough for a first down. On fourth-and-seven, Gilburg punted down to the Cleveland 31.

On first down, Brown punched out five yards up the middle. Momentum had been leaning toward Cleveland throughout the game, and now gave way with a mighty burst. On second down, Cleveland lined up in a double wing formation, which meant that Ernie Green lined up as a flanker to provide extra blocking while Jim Brown stayed in the backfield by himself. At the snap, Ryan pitched to Brown as Monte Clark and Gene Hickerson pulled out to lead the blocking. Brown ran past two defenders while Hickerson and Clark each knocked a man out of the way. At the Baltimore 30, Jerry Logan caught up to Brown as he cut toward the middle of the field. Logan dove for Brown's legs, and brought him down on the 18 after gaining 47 yards.

With their best field position of the game, the Browns looked to get into the end zone. Ryan at first thought about going back to the run, but felt the Colts might be looking for it. He decided to mix things up with a pass, and called Cleveland's bread-and-butter play, the post-pattern to Collins.

While Ryan was setting up in the pocket, Collins attempted to make his way through the defense. At this time, the Colts got their defensive signals crossed up, and the man who was supposed to drop deep into the middle zone went to the outside instead. Collins was covered at first along the sideline, but once he broke across the middle, there was no defender in the area. Ryan let the ball go as pressure was coming in fast from tackle Fred Miller. The ball went under the crossbar of the goal post and into the hands of a wide-open Collins for a touchdown. With Groza's conversion, the Browns were up, 10-0, as Cleveland Stadium erupted with excitement.

Lorick received Groza's kickoff two yards deep in the end zone, and decided to bring it out. After getting to the 11, Lorick was met with a bone-jarring hit by Leroy Kelly. Adding to Baltimore's grief was the fact that they were called for clipping on the run back, and would have to start their drive on the 5. After moving only seven yards, Gilburg punted, and once again he got off a terrible kick. This time he hooked it into the wind, and it went out of bounds on the Baltimore 39.

Ryan gave the ball to Warfield on a reverse to get things going, but Bob Boyd shot through to tackle him for a 3-yard loss. On second-and-thirteen from the 42, Cleveland lined up in a strong left formation. Jerry Logan misread the alignment and went into the coverage area for anything short to the outside. What he should

have done in a strong left formation was drop deep to cover the middle. At the snap, Logan quickly went to the outside while Collins saw the unprotected area that Logan should have been in. With his blocking doing a tremendous job, Ryan had all day to wait for Collins to get to the right spot. With the wind at his back, Ryan threw a beautiful pass that found Collins on the six, and the receiver crossed the goal line untouched for his second touchdown catch of the day. Groza's conversion followed and Cleveland was looking like they were about to shock the football world, as they were now up 17-0.

The ensuing kickoff went out of the end zone, and the Colts once again had to start a series from their 20-yard line. With time running out in the third quarter, Unitas desperately looked to get something going. He connected with Berry on first down for four yards. After allowing Baltimore to pick up two first downs, the Browns tightened down. On third down, Unitas' pass fell incomplete, but a defensive holding penalty gave the Colts the ball on the Cleveland 48. That was the only joy that Baltimore could muster, because Moore fumbled on the next play, and Wiggin recovered. As the third quarter came to a close, the Browns were on the Baltimore 14 thanks to a 22-yard run by Brown.

Up to this time, rookie sensation Paul Warfield was held without a reception. Aware that he was a dangerous threat, the Colts shut him down with double coverage. On the first play of the fourth quarter, however, Ryan managed to finally get one to the rookie. Warfield cut across the middle right in front of the goal posts and caught Ryan's pass on the 1, but was denied a touchdown when

Lyles hauled him down just shy of the goal line.

It was apparent to the Colts that Cleveland would call on Brown this close to the end zone. Twice the great fullback blasted into the line, and twice he came away defeated. The proud Colts knew at this stage of the game that they were beaten, but felt that stopping Brown this close to the goal line would give them some sense of pride on an otherwise brutal day. Facing third down, Ryan once again called on Brown. This time Brown vaulted himself right over the top of the pile. Linebacker Bill Pellington met him while he was airborne and cut into his legs. Brown still tried to get over by grabbing hold of the goal post in an attempt to pull himself over. It clearly looked like Brown had broken the plane of the goal line, but the officials ruled otherwise. After what many felt was a bad call by the officials, Groza kicked a chip shot field goal from the 9-yard line to increase the lead to 20-0.

There was no let up by the Cleveland defense. In Baltimore's next offensive series, Unitas was sacked twice, with Kanicki getting the first, and Glass and Wiggin sharing the other. The drive ended after five plays with Walter Roberts taking Gilburg's punt on the Cleveland 36.

Five runs by Brown, and a pass to Brewer got Cleveland to midfield. From his own 49, Ryan called on Collins one more time. At the snap, Collins took off deep, then hooked toward the middle with Bob Boyd staying with him step for step. Ryan made a beautiful throw into the wind that Collins caught off his shoulder pad at the 14 with Boyd hanging on him. After the catch, Boyd lost his footing and fell. Lyles and Logan gave chase, but

Collins got away from them to go into the end zone for a championship game record third touchdown reception. He was instantly mobbed in the end zone by delirious fans in the bleachers, and for a moment all that could be seen of Collins was the top of his helmet. Groza's extra point closed out the scoring at 27-0.

Beside setting a new championship game record with three touchdown receptions, Gary Collins was the overwhelming choice for the game's Most Valuable Player award. On the day he caught five passes for 130 yards.

Walter Beach secured the shutout by intercepting Unitas two plays after Groza's kickoff. This was Unitas' worst day as a pro. He completed 12 of 20 passes, which was good, but for only 95 yards, and he suffered two interceptions.

The rest of the game belonged to Cleveland, with Ryan killing the clock by handing off to Brown and Green. With 26 seconds left, Cleveland Municipal Stadium was turned into a frenzy, as fans stormed the field to tear down the goal posts. With the game far out of reach, the officials didn't even try to restore order, and called the game.

This was a true David vs. Goliath story. The 1964 Cleveland Browns did the impossible by executing perfectly on both sides of the ball to produce the most lopsided win by an underdog in NFL championship game history. To pull an upset is shocking enough, but one of this magnitude is just unbelievable.

Maybe everyone was right to call the '64 Browns the "Laugh Champs", because every person affiliated with the organization was surely laughing by nightfall on this cold December day in Cleveland.

BROWNS PLAY IN FIRST-EVER MONDAY NIGHT GAME

[SEPTEMBER 21, 1970]

On a hot, windless late summer evening in Cleveland, history was made on the shores of Lake Erie. At 9:00 p.m. on Monday, September 21, 1970, over 30 million viewers heard legendary sports announcer Howard Cosell's voice welcome them to the debut of Monday Night Football from Cleveland Municipal Stadium.

Even though Monday Night Football is regarded today as a phenomenal success week in and week out, it didn't start out that way when NFL commissioner Pete Rozelle came up with the idea prior to the 1970 season.

Rozelle will go down in professional sports history as the greatest commissioner to ever govern a league. He was an innovator who made the NFL the success story that it is today, and that it will be well into the future. Going into his eleventh season as commissioner in 1970, Rozelle came up with the idea of prime time football as a way to attract new fans and advertising dollars.

The opponents of Rozelle's concept didn't feel that sports on television would work during the week on a regular basis. They felt that on weekends, men watched sports in great numbers, and that made the three major networks very successful and rich. The weekdays, they felt, were more for family viewing, and didn't think that an extra night of football would be popular, and if it wasn't well received, there wouldn't be advertising money coming in.

Rozelle was still determined to sell his idea to the three major networks (ABC, CBS, and NBC). Right from the start, CBS and NBC said no. They were locked into that time slot with successful shows that made a lot of money for them, and were not willing to change a sure thing for something that was unknown and seemed destined to fail.

Over at ABC, Roone Arledge was the network's president of sports broadcasting, and he liked the idea. He knew the infatuation that people had with football, and believed in Rozelle's notion that it could be a success if done right. The only problem was that his bosses felt the same way as CBS and NBC.

With the three major networks rejecting him, Rozelle turned to billionaire Howard Hughes. Hughes owned a sports network, and Rozelle told ABC that he was going to sell the idea of Monday Night Football to Hughes. Once the ABC executives heard that a man of Hughes' status was interested in the concept, they gave it a little more thought, and finally agreed to give it a try for three years.

With his network now committed, Arledge set out on a quest to turn the new idea into a show that would be fun to watch. Before Monday Night Football, the broadcasts of football games were cut and dry. There was a play-by-play man and a color commentator, and their banter was strictly football. Arledge set out to change all that by having three men in the booth who could also be entertaining to listen to.

Arledge found his trio in the likes of Howard Cosell, Don Meredith, and Keith Jackson. In Cosell, the viewer had someone who was outspoken, cocky, and very opinionated. Cosell was a highly intelligent man who was never afraid to show his brilliance. He was a person the average fan just loved to hate. Next there was color man Don Meredith, who came into the broadcasting booth after retiring from a nine-year career as quarterback of the Dallas Cowboys in 1968. He was a laid-back Texan with an incredible sense of humor. His stories added flare to the show, and everyone loved it when he put Cosell in his place from time to time. He was probably the most entertaining color commentator pro football ever had. The hardest job in the booth was probably that of Keith Jackson, who had to give the play-by-play, and also keep an eye on the antics of Cosell and Meredith. Jackson

only lasted that first season, and was replaced in 1971 by Frank Gifford.

When it came time to schedule the games for the 1970 season, nobody wanted to be on Monday Night Football's first broadcast. Most owners felt that it would be a financial failure for their organizations to play a game on a week night. They didn't think that many people would turn out on a work day, so the owners weren't willing to risk a bad gate.

Art Modell stepped up to say that the Cleveland Browns would host the first Monday Night game. He didn't have to worry about fan support, because Browns' fans could always be counted on to come out to the stadium in great numbers regardless of the day. Before this game, the Browns had eight straight home crowds of 80,000 or better. It also didn't hurt to have the second largest seating capacity in the NFL. Arledge knew that a big turnout would be just what was needed to hook the country in each week. Arledge didn't have to worry about people not showing up, as 85,703 turned out to set the all-time Cleveland record. An additional 2,000 were turned away at the gate.

Opposing the Browns on that summer evening were the New York Jets and their flashy quarterback, Joe Namath. Two years earlier, Namath led the Jets to victory over the highly favored Baltimore Colts in Super Bowl III, which still stands as one of the greatest upsets in all of sports. Namath was at the peak of his career coming into this game, and his popularity around the country only helped ABC's chances. He was a master at play calling, and possessed one of the strongest arms in football history. This time period in Jets history was the franchise's most successful, and they were picked as one of the teams to win the Super Bowl. Coaching the team was former Browns' assistant Weeb Ewbank. After being let go by Baltimore after the 1962 season, Ewbank was hired the following season by the Jets.

The Browns were also one of the better teams in football, and were coming off two straight NFL championship game appearances. With two good teams looking to establish themselves early in the season, this game had all the makings of a classic battle.

Beside the debut of Monday Night Football, there was also another reason for excitement on this evening. Since 1960, there were two leagues in professional football. The American Football League was born in that year, and after a few seasons, began to challenge the NFL for fan support. No other league had given the NFL such a fight as the AFL did. Unlike the other leagues that challenged the NFL before, the AFL had money and television contracts, and were not going to go away like the other leagues did. Aware that something had to be done, the NFL asked the AFL to merge with them into one league in 1966.

The AFL accepted and officially merged at the start of the 1970 season with common schedules and playoffs. Until 1970, the leagues remained separate, but played a championship game at the end of the season between the winners of the NFL and AFL. This was how the Super Bowl was born. After the 1969 season, the National Football League was divided into two conferences, with the AFL teams being placed in the American Conference, and the NFL's teams in the National Conference.

When it came time for the merger to take place, the NFL had 16 teams and the AFL 10. The AFL representatives wanted a balanced conference, but the NFL owners wanted to leave things as they were, and let the AFL catch up through expansion.

With much bickering on both sides, it was Art Modell who once again stepped up with a solution to balance things out. Modell said he was willing to take the Browns into the American Conference along with St. Louis and Pittsburgh. Modell would not go, however, without Pittsburgh, because he didn't want to break up one of football's classic rivalries. Pittsburgh's Art Rooney went along with the plan, but St. Louis' owners refused. After more bickering, it was decided that Baltimore would join the AFC to give both conferences 13 teams each. The Browns and Steelers joined Cincinnati and Houston to form the Central Division of the AFC, while Baltimore entered the AFC Eastern Division.

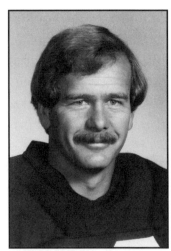

Don Cockroft

With the temperature a humid 80 degrees, Don Cockroft started a new era in pro football by sending the opening kickoff into the windless sky. With millions of eyes watching, the Jets took over possession, but failed to create much excitement in their opening drive. They couldn't move the ball, and Cleveland took over on their own 45 after New York punted.

The Browns wasted little time bringing the overflow crowd to its feet, as quarterback Bill Nelsen took Cleveland 55 yards in nine plays. Attacking a young New York secondary, Nelsen drove the Browns to the 8, and from there, he made Gary Collins the answer to a trivia question by throwing a touchdown pass to him for the first-ever score on Monday Night Football. Cockroft added the extra point, and Cleveland had an early 7-0 lead.

Nelsen got the ball back within a few minutes, and this time guided the Browns 84 yards on eleven plays, with running back Bo Scott finished the drive off with a sweep around the left side from the 2. Cleveland was helped on the drive by two pass interference penalties. Cockroft's conversion increased the led to 14-0 at the end of the first quarter.

The Jets looked to get back in the game after a 38-yard kickoff return by Mike Battle. With guard Randy Rasmussen handling rookie defensive tackle Jerry Sherk with ease, New York's backfield of Matt Snell and Emerson Boozer began to run well. The Jets covered 61 yards in eight plays, and Boozer put New York on the board with a 2-yard run. Jim Turner's conversion closed the gap to 14-7.

New York continued to gather momentum and they found themselves on the Cleveland 17 late in the second quarter. Namath tried to get the Jets tied up, and threw a pass intended for receiver George Sauer, but defensive back Walt Sumner made a leaping interception to kill the drive. With time almost expired in the first half, Namath took one more stab at the end zone, but linebacker Jim Houston cut in front of tight end Pete Lammons for another interception.

Homer Jones was a fast receiver obtained by Cleveland from the New York Giants prior to the 1970 season. He only played with the Browns for one season, but made an impact by being the first player to return a kickoff for a touchdown on Monday Night Football. He took Turner's kickoff on the 6 to start the second half. After gaining speed behind good blocking, Jones went up the right sideline, cut to the middle, then switched to full acceleration. He outran two defenders to the end zone, and Cockroft's conversion gave the Browns back their 14-point cushion at 21-7.

New York came back with Boozer scoring his second touchdown of the game, this time from 10 yards out. Cockroft added a 27-yard field goal to end the third quarter with Cleveland leading, 24-14.

Both teams had problems early in the fourth quarter. Cockroft missed an easy 18-yard field goal, and Matt Snell fumbled after New York had reached the Cleveland 7. On first down, Namath and Snell got their signals mixed up. At the snap, Namath thought Snell was going wider, and reached out farther with the ball on the handoff exchange. Snell was on his way to the inside, and couldn't adjust in time when going into the line. The confusion resulted in a fumble that defensive end Jack Gregory recovered. The Browns didn't score on the drive, but they did knock six minutes off the clock before giving it back to the Jets.

The next time Namath got his hands on the ball, he wasted no time. In just four plays, all of them passes, Broadway Joe took his Jets 80 yards for a touchdown. From the Cleveland 33, Namath threw to Sauer for a touchdown as the

Browns were coming in on a blitz. Sauer made a great catch with defensive back Fred Summers right on him. Turner's conversion made it a 24-21 game with plenty of time left for Namath to pull out a victory.

The momentum was starting to swing the Jets' way, and their inspired defense held the Browns on their next possession. On Cockroft's punt, the Browns received a huge break when Battle signaled for a fair catch at the New York 30, but let the ball go past him. The ball rolled all the way to the 4 before Cleveland downed it, putting the Jets in a huge hole and killing their momentum.

With less than a minute to play, Namath still looked to pull out a heroic come-from-behind victory. He was off on a good start toward his quest, as he took the Jets to the Cleveland 25. Looking for Sauer from there, Namath fired a pass in his receiver's direction, but right outside linebacker Billy Andrews stepped in front of Sauer to intercept. Andrews wasn't stopped on the return, and sealed the victory for Cleveland with a 25-yard touchdown to make the final score, 31-21.

The Jets dominated Cleveland everywhere but on the scoreboard. They doubled the Browns' offensive total, 455 yards to 221, but three interceptions were the killers for New York. Despite throwing those costly interceptions, Namath still shined by completing 19 of 32 passes for 299 yards. Matt Snell was also productive for New York, as his 108 yards on the ground led all ballcarriers.

More important than this game was the fact that Rozelle's dream, and Roone Arledge's innovations paid off big time. They put Monday Night Foot-ball on the screen, and it grew in popularity well beyond anyone's wildest dreams. Today, Monday Night Football is a big draw every week, and ranks as one of the longest running shows in television history.

As for the two teams who kicked off this football institution, they never lived up to their preseason expectations. The Jets fell apart when Joe Namath broke his wrist, and Matt Snell tore his Achilles tendon. Nagging injuries to other key players put the Jets in a tailspin, and they never were a threat, finishing the season at 4-10. The Browns did a little better than the Jets, but still not good enough to make a run at a championship. They ended their season at 7-7 to finish one game out of first place in the AFC Central.

Billy Andrews

BROWNS' FIRST MEETING WITH PAUL BROWN AND THE CINCINNATI BENGALS

[OCTOBER 11, 1970]

When Paul Brown coached Cleveland to a 35-14 win over Pittsburgh on November 25, 1962 in the home finale, little did he know at the time that it would take him eight years to coach another game inside Cleveland Municipal Stadium.

After Brown was fired by Art Modell in 1963, he stayed away from pro football until the city of Cincinnati was granted a team in the AFL. Brown was coaxed back into the game by the Bengals in their inaugural season of 1968 as head coach and general manager.

In the Bengals' first two seasons, they were 7-20-1, but played their opponents tough with a roster loaded with inexperienced players and castoffs from other teams. Paul Brown molded and shaped his team through those first two seasons, and by 1970, they were on the verge of seeing his hard work pay off.

After knocking off a tough Oakland Raiders team in their opener, the Bengals suffered two straight losses coming into Cleveland on October 11.

Following their win in the first Monday Night game, the Browns split their next two, but were still in first place in the Central Division despite nagging injuries to key personnel.

Quarterback Bill Nelsen was plagued by bad knees when he came to the Browns in 1968, but could still get the job done. In both his

Paul Brown

previous seasons prior to 1970, Nelsen got the Browns into two straight NFL title games. The week leading up to Cincinnati's first-ever visit to Cleveland saw Nelsen miss practice throughout the week due to his knees, but by game day he was ready to go.

Joining Nelsen in the spectator section during workouts were his backfield mates, Leroy Kelly (sprained ankle), and Bo Scott (sore knee). Kelly took over for Jim Brown after the legendary runner retired in 1966, and immediately made his own impact on the NFL. In 1966, Kelly ran for 1,141 yards and a league high 15 rushing touchdowns. In 1967 his 1,205 yards and 11 touch-

Bill Nelsen

downs led the NFL, as did his 1,239 yards and 16 touchdowns in 1968. Scott was in his second year, and was starting to come into his own as the team's fullback.

A standing-room-only crowd of 83,520 were present to witness the first-ever battle of Ohio on a dismal October afternoon.

Cincinnati took early advantage of penalties, poor pass coverage, and a banged-up Cleveland backfield, to jump out to a 10-0 lead. Soccer-style kicker Horst Muhlmann got the Bengals on the board first with a whopping 50-yard field goal. Running back Jess Phillips added the other first quarter Cincinnati points with a 2-yard run.

Cleveland cut the lead to 10-2 when massive defensive tackle Walter Johnson crashed through the line and dropped quarterback Virgil Carter in the end zone for a safety. This was Carter's first start for the Bengals, and the Cleveland defense gave him an Ohio welcome by sacking him four more times throughout the game.

Bill Nelsen and his injured companions managed to get their sore joints going in the early stages of the second quarter. From the Bengals' 3, Nelsen threw a touchdown to Kelly, and Don Cockroft added the extra point to close the gap to 10-9.

Defensive end Royce Berry applied heavy pressure on Nelsen throughout the game, and on one occasion, caused him to fumble. While looking for Collins, Nelsen was hit by Berry as he was ready to release the ball and fumbled. Berry picked it up and ran 58 yards for a touchdown to give the Bengals a 17-9 lead.

The Browns rebounded when Leroy Kelly caught a Nelsen pass and went 55 yards to set the Browns up deep in Cincinnati territory. Nelsen finished the drive off with a 4-yard pass to tight end Milt Morin, and Cockroft's conversion made it 17-16 at halftime.

The Bengals increased their lead to 20-16 in the third quarter on Muhlmann's 23-yard field goal. The score remained that way throughout the rest of the quarter, but the Browns started moving the ball with authority near the end of the quarter.

In the opening minutes of the fourth quarter, Kelly put Cleveland in the lead for the first time by sweeping around the end from 1 yard out. Cockroft's extra point put the Browns up, 23-20.

Momentum began to shift over to the Browns at this point, and Erich Barnes helped the cause by intercepting a pass on the Cincinnati 26, and returning it to the 6-yard line. Two plays later, running behind the blocking of Gene Hickerson, Bo Scott scored from 1 yard out to put Cleveland up, 30-20. He then took himself out of the game following the touchdown due to his bad knee. After cutting on it all afternoon, the knee was sore, and Scott didn't want to push the tender joint too hard.

The Bengals rallied moments later with a nine-play, 75-yard drive that was climaxed by a Carter-to-Speedy Thomas touchdown pass from the Cleveland 16. Muhlmann's conversion made it 30-27 with plenty of time left for the Bengals to pull out a win.

Bo Scott

The Browns looked to run as much time off the clock as possible from this point on, but Cincinnati's defense dug in, and had Cleveland in a third-and-five situation on their own 38-yard line with 1:50 remaining.

The Bengals called a time out, and Nelsen took advantage of it to confer with Blanton Collier and assistant Nick Skorich on what to do in this situation. The unanimous decision was for Nelsen to throw. On the biggest play of the drive, Nelsen went to Cleveland's go-to guy for many years, Gary Collins, who came through like so many times before. His sideline catch for eight yards allowed Cleveland to keep possession until ten seconds remained.

The Bengals got possession following a fourth-down punt, and had time for only one play. Everyone knew that Virgil Carter was going to throw, and when he dropped back, the Browns' front line came crashing in on him with reckless abandon. Defensive end Jack Gregory got to Carter first and sacked him for a loss of 12 yards.

As both teams were making their way to the locker rooms, Collier went to midfield in an attempt to shake Paul Brown's hand, which is a customary ritual among coaches. Brown did not make any attempt to go toward Collier, and just kept walking to the tunnel. Most of the huge crowd witnessed Brown's evasiveness, and began to boo loudly as he walked by.

It looked to everyone like Brown was being a sore loser, and was still enraged about his firing. It would have been a safe bet to say that Brown carried some animosity toward the Cleveland organization for the rest of his life, but what the crowd saw was not a blowoff on Brown's part. In fact, Brown didn't shake hands after a game for many years prior to his return to Cleveland Stadium as an enemy. During Brown's days in Cleveland, the NFL sent out a message to league coaches calling for the elimination of the postgame handshake. The reasoning was that there might have been a problem during the game between opposing coaches, and once they walked toward each other, punches could start flying, and the possibility of a riot occurring were very good. Brown decided to follow the NFL's request, even though most coaches did not.

What the crowd must not have seen before the game started was Brown and Collier talking to each other near the Cincinnati bench. Collier put his arm around Brown, and the two longtime friends shared pleasantries with each other. Maybe Collier was so used to shaking hands at the end of a game, that he forgot Brown's policy, but whatever the reason, the bottom line was that Cleveland won the game, and were atop the Central Division at 3-1, while the Bengals slipped to 1-3.

In the end, however, it was Paul Brown who came out victorious in the division race. After this game, the Bengals went 7-3, and the Browns 4-6. Along the way to the Central Division title, Brown and his Bengals evened the score with Cleveland by beating them 14-10 down in Cincinnati.

THE KARDIAC KIDS

[1978–1980]

When Sam Rutigliano was hired as head coach of the Cleveland Browns on December 28, 1977, little did he know that over the course of the next three seasons his heart and blood pressure were going to endure a lot of wear and tear. Rutigliano did not go through his suffering alone, because an entire city's cardiovascular system took a beating right along with coach Sam's whenever the Kardiac Kids took the field from 1978 to 1980.

In the 48 regular season games played by the Browns during this time period, 24 of them were not decided until the closing seconds, and 17 of them were won by Cleveland.

Throughout the long and successful history of the Browns, many memories surround the championships won, but not like the ones created by the Kardiac Kids, even though they never won a league title. Over the three seasons that they were called the Kardiac Kids, the Browns were 28-20, and won the Central Division in 1980, but made an early exit from the Super Bowl race following that season in a divisional playoff loss to Oakland. Despite never winning the Super Bowl, or ever coming close, this still remains one of the most romantic times in team history. The excitement level week after week captivated the entire city of Cleveland, and even people with very little interest in football got swept up in the frenzy.

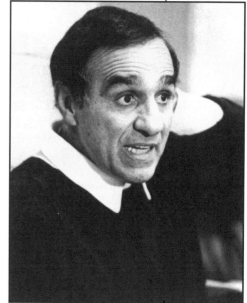

Sam Rutigliano

It could have been that beside the fact of being exciting to watch, the Kardiac Kids were all Cleveland really had as far as anything close to a winner at the time. Unlike the times when the Browns shared the championship spotlight with baseball's Cleveland Indians, and hockey's Cleveland Barons, the Kardiac Kids stood alone for the most part in fan admiration. At that time (1978-80), the Indians were perennial losers who resided in the basement of the American League. The original Barons left town in the early 70s, and were reborn later in the decade, only to become the worst team in the National Hockey League. After two disastrous seasons, they fled to a different location. Rounding out the sorry state of Cleveland sports during this time were the Cavaliers of the National Basketball Association. After some success in the mid-70s, the Cavs, like the Indians and Barons, were stuck in the lowest echelon of their sport at the end of the decade.

Regardless of why the Kardiac Kids were so loved, and still are to this day by all who lived through it, they rank right up there with the championship teams in Browns' history. Let us go back now to that time, and relive those 17 victories that stopped the hearts of all who loved the Kardiac Kids:

September 10, 1978:

The Browns were real bad throughout three quarters, then got real good when it counted most in a 13-10 overtime win over Cincinnati in sweltering heat. They fell behind, 10-0, then began to rally late in the third quarter.

Quarterback Brian Sipe suffered through four sacks and a whole lot of booing from 72,000 fans in Cleveland for poor play, especially in the second and third quarters. Despite his poor showing

Brian Sipe got sacked four times, but still managed to pass for 219 yards in Cleveland's 1978 victory over Cincinnati.

in those quarters, Sipe managed to put together a good game, completing 16 out of 32 passes for 219 yards. He had one touchdown pass, and it was a big one. With 10:17 left in regulation, Sipe fired a 13-yard scoring strike to Reggie Rucker that tied the game after Don Cockroft's conversion.

The game went into overtime after Bengals kicker Chris Bahr hooked a 37-yard field goal attempt with no time left on the clock.

The Browns won the coin toss for the overtime period, and rookie Larry Collins returned the kickoff 41 yards to midfield to give Cleveland excellent field position to start with. With Greg and Mike Pruitt running the ball, and rookie tight end Ozzie Newsome making a key sideline catch, the Browns quickly got to the Cincinnati 13. On third-and-five, Rutigliano didn't want to wait any longer, and sent in the field goal unit. A hush fell over the huge crowd as Cockroft's foot met the ball, but seconds later the stadium erupted as his kick split the uprights from 27 yards out to give the Browns the win with four-and-a-half minutes gone in overtime.

September 17, 1978:

The Browns stayed perfect under Rutigliano, as they beat Atlanta, 24-16, to go 3-0. For the second straight week, the Browns played in sweltering conditions, with the temperature climbing in to the 90s down in Atlanta.

With seven minutes left in the fourth quarter, the Falcons closed to within one point at 17-16. The Browns then drove down to the Atlanta 11 before losing a fumble. Falcons' quarterback Steve Bartkowski looked to put his team in the lead by going deep with 4:42 left. Defensive back Thom Darden killed the drive by intercepting the long pass.

Cleveland then went on a nine-play, 52-yard drive that ate up over three minutes, and provided the clincher with 1:19 showing on the clock. The deciding touchdown came on a Brian Sipe 2-yard quarterback sneak, but it wasn't supposed to be that way. The ball was supposed to go to Cleo Miller on a handoff, but Sipe fumbled the snap from center. A big break happened when the ball didn't start bouncing all over the place, but just laid on the ground motionless. This enabled the quick-thinking Sipe to pick it up and run for the score.

November 19, 1978:

The Baltimore Colts dominated this game until the middle of the second quarter by taking advantage of a struggling Cleveland offense, and were up, 10-0.

The Browns then came back with their best offensive production in a decade to run away from the Colts, 45-24. Changing from a running game, Sipe began to gamble with long passes in the second quarter, and it paid off for the rest of the game. He completed 15 of 22 passes for 309 yards and four touchdowns, three of which went to Calvin Hill. Reggie Rucker caught the other one. The win gave the Browns a 6-6 record, and put them back in the playoff picture.

Calvin Hill

Reggie Rucker

December 12, 1978:

The Browns were erased from the playoff picture in a loss to Seattle before they met the New York Jets on an ugly afternoon in Cleveland.

The Jets were still in the playoff hunt, and rebounded from a 27-10 fourth quarter Cleveland lead, to go into the final 1:11 up, 34-27.

After scoring their go-ahead touchdown, the Jets kicked off to Larry Collins, who brought the ball out to the Cleveland 27. Brian Sipe then began to work his magic, and hit on four of five passes to get the Browns to the New York 44 with 29 seconds left. Sipe was red hot, and looked to continue attacking through the air. On the following play, he threw a perfect pass into the corner of the end zone which Calvin Hill caught for a touchdown. Don Cockroft's conversion tied the game up with 20 seconds left in regulation, and the Browns were headed to their third overtime game of the season.

Sam Rutigliano

Cleveland won the coin toss, and Greg Pruitt followed with one of the most productive drives of his career. After taking the kickoff 31 yards to the New York 49, Pruitt carried the ball three straight times for a total of 44 yards. Two plays later from the 5, Cockroft won his second overtime game of the season, this time with a 22-yard field goal at the 3:07 mark. The Browns 37-34 win gave them an 8-7 record, and also eliminated the Jets from playoff contention.

A week later the Browns were blown out, 48-16, in Cincinnati to finish the season at .500.

September 2, 1979:

The Kardiac Kids started things off in 1979 with a heart-stopping 25-22 overtime win at the expense of the New York Jets. The Jets scored a touchdown that tied the game at 19-19 with 4:48 left in the fourth quarter, but kicker Pat Leahy missed the extra point.

The normally sure-handed Ricky Feacher fumbled a kickoff against the Jets in 1979.

extremely poised under pressure.

Starting from his own 14, Sipe drove the Browns into field goal range. His throw to Dave Logan put the Browns close enough for Don Cockroft to hit a 35-yarder with four seconds left to force the game into overtime. Sipe was brilliant in this opener, completing 21 of 36 passes for 302 yards and a touchdown. Logan was Sipe's main receiver with six receptions for 115 yards. Greg and Mike Pruitt also helped out offensively with a solid running attack.

With 35 seconds left in overtime, New York quarterback Matt Robinson was rushed while looking for an open receiver. Throughout this game, the Cleveland defense was relentless in their pursuit of Robinson. Led by Lyle Alzado, the defense sacked Robinson five times, and looked to be ready to do it again when he threw a hurried pass on third-and-ten from his 38-yard line. The pass was intended for Clark Gianes, but was intercepted by Oliver Davis on the Cleveland 36, and returned to the New York 31.

With 24 seconds left in the overtime period, Sipe connected with Logan on the Jets' 21, and he ran out of bounds to stop the clock. Rutigliano sent Cockroft in with 18 seconds left, and once again, the kicker came through. This time it was from 27 yards out, and the Browns had a 25-22 win.

Leahy got a chance to redeem himself quickly, as Ricky Feacher fumbled the ensuing kickoff, and New York recovered on the Cleveland 23. Thanks to a tough Cleveland defense, the Jets failed to get into the end zone in five plays, but Leahy hit on a 21-yard field goal to give New York what looked like the winning points with 1:58 left.

The Browns were starting to get used to being in these situations, and they calmly went about doing what they had to do. With Brian Sipe at the controls, the Browns knew that anything was possible. He was coming into his own as one of the premier quarterbacks in the NFL, and was

September 9, 1979:

Getting the reputation of having nerves of steel, Sipe once again pulled out a win in the closing seconds. This time it was against the Kansas City Chiefs, 27-24, with the winning points coming with 52 seconds remaining in the game.

The Browns lost a 20-0 lead with 5:30 left after the Chiefs went up, 21-20. Sipe had a great day throwing (19 of 35 for 243 yards), but threw an interception which led to a 30-yard field goal by Jan Stenerud.

Things looked bleak when the Browns got the ball back trailing 24-20, and Kansas City owning all the momentum. It didn't stay somber for long, as Sipe took the Browns from the Cleveland 24 to the Kansas City 21 in six plays. Two plays later, Sipe found Reggie Rucker in the end zone to pull out a 27-24 win.

September 16, 1979:

It looked like Cleveland's Kardiac Kids' finishes were becoming a ritual. For the third straight week of the '79 season, the Browns went down to the wire to win a nailbitter and remain undefeated.

This time it was winless Baltimore who were their victims, after the Colts had jumped out to a 10-0 lead in the first ten minutes. Once again Sipe was the man. With three minutes left in the fourth quarter, and the game tied at 10-10, Sipe launched a bomb to Ozzie Newsome from the Cleveland 10. The play covered 74 yards, and set the Browns up on the Baltimore 16. Four plays later, Cockroft's 28-yard field goal split the uprights with 1:51 to go to give the Browns a 13-10 win.

Lyle Alzado

October 21, 1979:

Unable to move the ball in the first half, the Browns fell behind Cincinnati, 20-7, in the third quarter. With Mike Pruitt's running, and Brian Sipe's passing, Cleveland got things going. Sipe took the Browns to a touchdown in 12 plays that covered 80 yards. He ended the drive with a 2-yard pass to Ricky Feacher.

On the first play following a Dino Hall punt return that gave the Browns the ball at midfield, Sipe threw to Mike Pruitt across the middle. After getting a block, Pruitt ran to the sidelines and went the distance. With Cockroft's conversion, the Browns were in the lead for the first time, 21-20. Pruitt had one of his best days in a Cleveland uniform. He led all rushers with 135 yards, and caught four passes.

Cleveland increased their lead to 28-20 when Sipe threw his fourth touchdown of the day, a 27-yarder to Newsome.

The Bengals looked to get back into the game after seeing their commanding lead crumble. They closed the Cleveland lead to one point by going on a 4-play, 75-yard drive that was capped off by Pete Johnson's 32-yard run with 6:26 left in the fourth.

Cincinnati stopped the Cleveland offense on their next possession, and forced a punt, but just as return man Scott Burk touched the ball, Feacher nailed him, causing a fumble. Feacher recovered for the Browns on the Cincinnati 39.

The Bengals regained possession after Cockroft missed a field goal with 1:48 remaining. After completing one pass, quarterback Ken Anderson was sacked, and then a fourth down pass was batted down. Sipe took over on downs, and ran the final seconds off the clock for a great come-from-behind victory that gave the Browns a 5-3 record.

November 4, 1979:

With four minutes left in the fourth quarter, the Philadelphia Eagles were winning, 19-10, and looked like a sure bet to send their fans home happy. Unfortunately, the Eagles were playing the Browns, and being down with little time left meant nothing to them.

The Browns' good fortune began when Eagles' running back Wilbert Montgomery fumbled for the second time in the game, and linebacker Clay Mathews recovered on the Philadelphia 29.

The Eagles quickly went into a "prevent" defense to guard against Sipe's much-feared passing arm. Knowing the defense would be looking for the pass, Sipe mixed things up by handing off to Dino Hall, who shocked the Eagles with a 24-yard pickup. On the next play, Sipe went to the air, and found Newsome for the touchdown from five yards out. The scoring drive took only 52 seconds, and Cockroft's extra point made the score 19-17 with 3:21 left.

The Cleveland defense held the Eagles on their next possession, and got the ball back into Sipe's hands with 2:12 remaining. In four plays, the Browns got the ball into field goal range. Then the Eagles once again shifted into the "prevent" defense, and Sipe kept the ball on the ground. With the ball on the Philadelphia 24, the Eagles looked for Sipe to switch back to the pass, and blitzed. Sipe picked up the blitz, and handed off to Mike Pruitt, who then ran through the unprotected area left vacant by the blitzing linebackers. Pruitt crossed the goal line with 48 seconds left, and following

Ozzie Newsome earned Pro Football Hall of Fame Honors in 1999.

Cockroft's conversion, the Browns were leading, 24-19.

The Eagles gave victory one final chance, and covered 75 yards in a hurry, but linebacker Charlie Hall saved the day for Cleveland with an interception on the Browns' 1-yard line to ice the game. This win gave the Browns a 7-3 record, and put them on the verge of gaining their first playoff appearance since 1972.

November 18, 1979:

Not too uncommon for the Browns, they found themselves down by seven points late in the game. This time it was the Miami Dolphins who had the best of them, 24-17, with 3:53 remaining in the game.

Also not uncommon for the Browns was the fact that Brian Sipe engineered another comeback, and registered another outstanding performance, completing 23 out of 42 passes for 358 yards and three touchdowns.

With 1:21 remaining, Sipe got Cleveland into the end zone with a 34-yard pass to a wide open Ozzie Newsome. Cockroft then put the game into overtime with the extra point that made it 24-24.

The Browns won the overtime coin toss, and Dino Hall brought the kickoff out to the Cleveland 26. On the first play, with his receivers covered, Sipe ran for nine yards. Mike Pruitt then carried for four yards and a first down on the 39. The Browns reached midfield on the next play when Sipe connected with Calvin Hill for 11 yards. Sipe was once again forced out of the pocket, and instead of hurting the Dolphins with his arm, he hurt them with his legs, as he picked up 11 yards.

After his run put the Browns on the Miami 39, Sipe called a timeout. Reggie Rucker approached Sipe during the timeout, and told him that he knew he could get open over the middle. Sipe listened to his receiver, and called his number in the huddle. At the snap, Rucker sliced his way between two defensive backs just as he said he could, and Sipe threw the ball the instant he saw Rucker break free. The receiver caught the pass with no opposition, and reached the end zone untouched to give Cleveland a 30-24 win.

The Browns saw themselves at 8-4 following this game, and only one game behind the Pittsburgh Steelers in the Central Division. The next weekend, the Browns traveled to Pittsburgh, but lost a heartbreaker, 33-30, in overtime. They rebounded against Houston, but losses in their final two games left them with a respectable 9-7 record, but not good enough to make the playoffs.

September 28, 1980:

The Browns won their second in a row to even their season record at 2-2 with a 34-27 victory over Tampa Bay. Cleveland was rolling along, 31-13, in the fourth quarter, and after Clinton Burrell intercepted a pass with 9:11 left, things looked good for the Browns. Tampa Bay refused to give up, and scored two touchdowns in the final six minutes to pull within seven points. With only seconds left on the clock, quarterback Doug Williams got the Bucs to the Cleveland 20. He threw to Jimmie Giles across the middle with no time-outs remaining instead of looking for someone near the sidelines. If Williams would have thrown to the sidelines, the receiver could have stepped out of bounds to stop the clock and give Tampa Bay one more shot at the end zone. Instead, Giles caught the ball on the 20 in the middle of the field with 12 seconds left. Giles was stopped, and the rest of the time ran off the clock to preserve the win.

October 19, 1980:

Just as they did in the Tampa Bay game, the Browns lost a lead, then had to scramble at the end to pull out a win. When looking back on the Kardiac Kids, these last second wins were what made them so special in our memories, but at the time they were grueling to watch. Such was the case against the Green Bay Packers, who the Browns had a 13-0 lead over, but found themselves down, 21-13, with 7:23 to go in the game.

Brian Sipe, as usual, played like the warrior he was, and closed the gap to 21-20 with a two-play, 69-yard drive. Sipe was hurting throughout the game due to a bad knee, sore ribs, and a tender elbow. No one would have known, however, because he hit on 24 of 39 passes for 391 yards and two touchdowns, with both coming in the final seven minutes of the game. The first was a 19-yard toss to Ozzie Newsome, and it came 28 seconds after the Packers scored their final touchdown. Calvin Hill got the Browns into position for the touchdown by taking a Sipe pass on the Cleveland 45, then out running several defenders for 50 yards until he was shoved out of bounds on the 19.

When the Packers got the ball back, they ate up four minutes with a sustained drive that took them from their 16 to the Browns' 43. On third-and-seven, Eddie Lee Ivery tried to get outside after taking a pitchout. Linebackers Robert L. Jackson and Charlie Hall dropped him after a gain of six, and forced the Packers to punt on fourth down with 1:53 left on the clock.

The Browns took over on their own 13 following the punt, and Sipe started the drive with a 15-yard pass to Hill. Sipe carried the ball himself on the next play for nine yards, and hurt his wrist on the play, but refused to come out of the game. Mike Pruitt carried for 11, then Sipe hit Hill for 16. With 49 seconds left, Sipe ran for 14 yards, but the play was called back due to a holding penalty. Sipe missed on the next two passes, and faced a third-and-twenty from the Green Bay 46. With 25 seconds left, Sipe dropped back on the critical down. He threw a high, lobbing pass toward Dave Logan while the receiver was covered. Logan was also a basketball star prior to playing pro football, and the pass looked like a rebound coming down off a backboard. Logan's basketball training paid off big time, as he outjumped the man covering him. After hauling in the pass on the 19, Logan resembled a snake by weaving his way through a flock of Packers until he crossed the goal line to put Cleveland up, 26-21. Cockroft's extra point attempt went wide to the left. Robert L. Jackson sealed the win with an interception in the final 13 seconds.

October 26, 1980:

For the first time in four years, the Browns beat the Pittsburgh Steelers. It marked their third straight win, and put them in a tie for first place with Houston in the Central Division.

The Steelers looked good early despite injuries to key offensive personnel. Capitalizing on turnovers, Pittsburgh held a 26-14 lead going in to the fourth quarter.

Sipe woke the Browns up from there with a ten-play, 73-yard drive. Three receptions by Dave Logan helped get the Browns inside the Pittsburgh 10. From the 7, Greg Pruitt came out of the backfield to catch his second touchdown pass of the day to make it 26-20 with 9:21 left. Cockroft missed the conversion.

When the Browns got the ball back, they went on a six-play, 60-yard drive to take the lead with 5:38 remaining. Sipe completed three passes in the short drive,

with the final one going for an 18-yard touchdown to Newsome. Cockroft nailed the extra point this time, and the Browns were up by the slimmest of margins, 27-26.

The Steelers took a shot at regaining the lead with 1:57 left. Stoudt tried to pass his team into field goal range, but Ron Bolton intercepted on the Cleveland 41. The Browns ran the clock down to 24 seconds following the interception, then punted on fourth down. Stoudt was sacked on first down, then connected with Jim Smith on the Cleveland 47 as the final seconds ran off.

November 9, 1980:
Playing their best offensive football of the season throughout the first half, the Browns took a 21-6 lead over the Baltimore Colts into the third quarter. Things changed at that point, as the Browns cooled off while Colts' quarterback Bert Jones got hot. He passed Baltimore to two touchdowns in the final minute-and-a-half to make the score 28-27. It looked like this one was going into overtime, but kicker Steve Mike-Mayer missed the conversion with 19 seconds left. Baltimore attempted an onside kick on the kickoff, and almost got possession back when Thom Darden bobbled the ball. Autry Beamon saved the day for Cleveland by fighting his way through several Colts to recover the ball and preserve the

Dave Logan

Browns' fifth win in a row.

November 30, 1980:
Cleveland went into Houston tied with the Oilers for first place in the Central Division at 8-4. Brian Sipe was the main star of the Kardiac Kids, but on this day, two unlikely heroes emerged to steal the headlines from the all-pro quarterback. Second-string fullback Cleo Miller led the team with 69 yards rushing, and scored both of Cleveland's touchdowns. He also set up what turned out to be the winning points with a 50-yard run in the third quarter. That run led to a Cockroft field goal that put the Browns up, 17-14 in the third quarter.

The other hero was defensive back Clarence Scott, who intercepted a Ken Stabler pass on the Cleveland 24 with 1:27 left in the game. Sipe downed the ball twice to kill the clock, and the Browns returned home in sole possession of first place with 10,000 screaming fans greeting them at the airport.

December 7, 1980:
The Browns blew a 10-0 lead, but came back on the brilliant passing of Sipe,

Greg Pruitt was one of the Browns' most exciting players.

to win their tenth game of the season for the first time since 1972. Sipe completed 30 of 41 passes for 340 yards, and one touchdown, which proved to be the game winner with 9:27 remaining in the game. Greg Pruitt was on the receiving end of the game winner. Returning to the lineup after missing several games due to a serious knee injury, Pruitt scored from five yards out after catching Sipe's pass. He caught 10 passes on the day, leaving him one shy of the team record.

The Jets reached midfield on their next possession in four plays, but stalled at that point. The Browns took over on their 8 following a punt, and got to midfield before the clock ran out.

December 21, 1980:

After a painful last-second Hail-Mary pass in Minnesota beat them in week 15, the Browns found themselves in a must-win situation going into their season finale down in Cincinnati. The Browns quickly saw their chances fading after the Bengals took advantage of a lethargic Cleveland offense to lead 10-0 in the second quarter. The Browns began to wake up as halftime grew near. A Sipe-to-Rucker touchdown pass, and a Cockroft field goal knotted the teams up at the intermission.

The Browns took a step backward 34 seconds into the third quarter when Sipe threw an interception to Ray Griffin that was returned for a 52-yard touchdown. Sipe redeemed himself later in the quarter by throwing two long touchdown passes to Ricky Feacher which put the Browns in the lead for the first time in the game at 24-17.

The Bengals refused to give the division title to Cleveland without a fight, and tied the game in the fourth quarter. For the final time while they were dubbed the Kardiac Kids, the Browns mounted a thrilling, game-winning drive. This time it

Ron Bolton

was a ten-play, 49-yard march that was highlighted by the running of Cleo Miller and Mike Pruitt that got the Browns deep into enemy territory. With 1:25 left on the clock, Cockroft hit a 22-yard field goal that gave the Browns a 27-24 lead.

The victory celebration did not begin after Cockroft's kick, because the Bengals still had enough time to get into position for either a tie or a win. It almost happened that way, as Cincinnati got down to the Cleveland 11 when time ran out. Ron Bolton saved the game, and the 1980 Central Division title by tackling Steve Kreider before he could get out of bounds to stop the clock.

One of the most exciting times in Cleveland Browns history came to an end on that December afternoon in Cincinnati. Two weeks later, the Kardiac Kids lost to the Oakland Raiders, 14-12, while driving for the winning points. On a play called, "Red-Right 88", Sipe threw to Ozzie Newsome in the end zone with only seconds left in the game. The ball looked to be headed for Newsome's hands, but defensive back Mike Davis cut in front of him to intercept, and with it bring an end to one exciting season.

The capacity crowd of over 80,000 in Municipal Stadium fell so silent that one could hear a pin drop at midfield. After the shock wore off, Clevelanders rebounded with the old cliché, "Wait till next year". Unfortunately, next year never came for the Kardiac Kids, and over the next five seasons, the Browns only had one winning record, with that being in 1983, when they went 9-7, but failed to make the playoffs. Even though the Kardiac Kids didn't win the Super Bowl, they won Cleveland's heart, and that's not a bad way to be remembered.

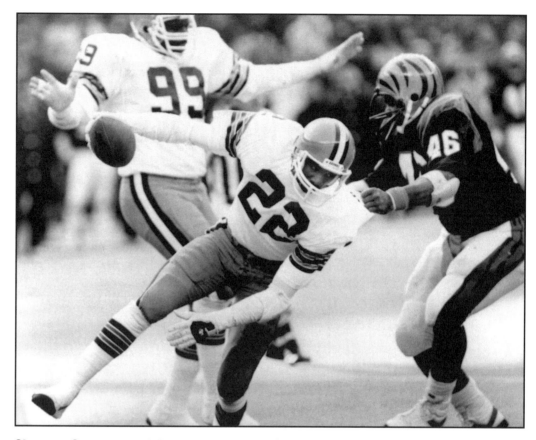

Clarence Scott was a defensive back from 1971-83.

THE BROWNS END THREE RIVER STADIUM JINX

[OCTOBER 5, 1986]

Jinxes. Some people believe in them while others laugh at such nonsense. In the case of Cleveland's misfortunes in Pittsburgh's Three Rivers Stadium throughout the 1970s and 80s, however, even the strongest skeptics of jinxes had to start pondering their existence.

From 1950 to 1969, the Browns owned the Pittsburgh Steelers. In the 40 games played between the two teams over the course of those twenty seasons, the Browns won 31 times. During that time, the Steelers played their home games at Forbes Field. In 1970, they moved into brand new Three Rivers Stadium, and that is when things got ugly for the Browns.

On November 29, 1970, the Browns traveled to Three Rivers Stadium for the first time, and got clobbered, 28-9. What seemed like a bad day for the Browns was only the beginning of their time in Hell with each visit made to Pittsburgh over a 15-year period.

In their first four trips to Three Rivers, the Browns couldn't even get more than nine points on the board each time they played there. The only excitement generated by Cleveland from 1970 through 1985 on their trips to Pittsburgh was when the Kardiac Kids played. In three visits, the Brian Sipe-led Browns forced the Steelers into overtime twice, in 1978 and 79, only to lose by a combined nine points.

The Cleveland organization was beside itself over the stigma. No matter how hard they played, it just wasn't good enough, and usually some turnover came at the most inopportune time to shift the momentum over to Pittsburgh. The Browns tried everything to break the jinx. Instead of traveling by plane, they rode in buses, stayed at different hotels, ate at different restaurants. Anything that could be changed from year to year was tried, but to no avail.

There could have been a jinx put on the Browns, but one simple thing held true during most of the years from 1970 to 1985, and that was the fact that the Steelers were one of the best teams in the NFL.

Former Clevelander and Browns player Chuck Noll was named head coach of the Steelers in 1969, and over the next decade, he took them from a 1-13 record to four time Super Bowl champs. The Steelers of that time are regarded by many historians as the greatest team to ever play the game. It seemed that the Browns could have played Pittsburgh anywhere during this time and lost.

By 1985, the tide started to turn in favor of the Browns. The once powerful Steelers had grown old and found themselves in a rebuilding period. The Browns on the other hand had suffered through dismal seasons during Pittsburgh's glory days, and by 1985 they were starting to come together as a team under new coach Marty Schottenheimer.

Marty Schottenheimer

After the Kardiac Kids lost to Oakland in the 1980 postseason, Sam Rutigliano suffered through a 5-11 season in 1981. The following year was a strike-shortened one that saw the Browns make the playoffs with a 4-5 record, and then get beat once again by the Raiders in the first round of the playoffs. In 1983, Rutigliano saw his team improve drastically to 9-7 in Brian Sipe's last season in Cleveland, but they failed to make it to the postseason. Rutigliano's coaching stay in Cleveland ended the next year after the Browns went 1-7 in the first half of the season. He was replaced by Schottenheimer, who guided the Browns to four wins in the final eight games.

In 1985, Schottenheimer led the Browns to an 8-8 record, but it was good enough in the weak Central Division to make them champions. They still lost in Three River Stadium, but this time it was by the closest of margins, 10-9. In a first-round playoff game down in Miami, the Browns led the heavily-favored Dolphins, 21-3, at the half, and were headed to one of the biggest upsets in NFL history. It would have made for a good story, but the Dolphins woke up in the second half to win, 24-21. Even in defeat, the Browns had to be proud of what they accomplished, and looked to 1986 as one of promise.

Led by second-year quarterback Bernie Kosar, the Browns went into

Former Browns player Chuck Noll held a longtime coaching jinx over Cleveland while he was Pittsburgh's coach.

Bernie Kosar

Cleveland's luck continued on the ensuing kickoff when return man Don Elder fumbled and Herman Fontenot recovered for Cleveland. Five plays later, kicker Matt Bahr was good from 22 yards out on a field goal attempt to give the Browns a 10-0 lead at the end of the first quarter.

It was at this time that the demons which so haunted the Browns in Pittsburgh awoke to torment them over the next three minutes. It started when Gerald McNeil dropped a long pass from Kosar with no one near him. If McNeil could have held on to the ball, it would have been a sure 80-yard touchdown reception, and a healthy lead for Cleveland. The next play proved to be more devastating when Kosar lost the ball while attempting to throw, and it was recovered by the Steelers on the Cleveland 10. The ball slipped out of his hand as he was moving his arm forward, which meant that he was in the act of throwing, and it should have been ruled an incomplete pass. The referee didn't see it that way, and neither did the instant replay official. Both parties ruled it a fumble, and gave Pittsburgh possession. Seven plays later,

Pittsburgh on October 5 with a 2-2 record. The Steelers were heading down a dark, lonely tunnel by 1986, losing three out of their first four games, and ending up with a 6-10 record. Many in the Cleveland organization felt that this was the year to end the Three River jinx, but they had that feeling before.

Things started off good for the Browns, as they scored first on a 15-yard pass from Kosar to wide receiver Webster Slaughter just two minutes into the first quarter. Slaughter's first NFL touchdown was helped along by a 53-yard pass interference call three plays earlier.

quarterback Mark Malone scored from 1 yard out to cut the lead to 10-7.

Wide receiver Reggie Langhorne was the next victim of the jinx when he fumbled after a gain of seven yards. The Steelers took over on the Cleveland 21, and took the lead four plays later on a Malone to Rich Erenberg 5-yard pass. The crowd was now feeling the momentum shift over to their beloved Steelers, and the noise throughout the stadium was ear-piercing.

McNeil made up for his dropped pass, and also quieted the crowd down briefly, by taking the ensuing kickoff 100 yards for a touchdown. It marked the first time since 1974 that a Cleveland player returned a kickoff for a score. Even better was the fact that McNeil's return took the Browns into half-time with a 17-14 lead.

Just as McNeil did his best to silence the crowd and put the Browns on top, it was his bobble of a punt on the Cleveland 34 nine minutes into the third quarter that brought the fans

back to life, and put the Steelers back in the lead, 21-17. The crowd noise became so intense that the Browns couldn't hear Kosar's signals for the rest of the game. It took Malone five plays to finish off the short drive, and he accomplished this by throwing his second touchdown of the day, this time to Louis Lipps from six yards out.

The following ten minutes of the game were brutal, smash-mouth football that was typical for these two blue collar

Gerald McNeil

teams. The Browns did manage to break through on one drive, and thanks to a 29-yard run by Earnest Byner, Cleveland got close enough for Bahr to kick a field goal from 39 yards to end the third quarter with Pittsburgh clinging to a slim 21-20 lead.

The Steelers came back in almost identical fashion as the Browns did on their last scoring drive. With 18 seconds expired in the fourth, Pittsburgh took a 24-20 lead after Gary Anderson hit on a 45-yard field goal. The three-pointer was set up when Earnest Jackson covered 25 yards on the ground in one burst.

The demons circling over the Cleveland sideline must have looked away briefly when a punt taken by Rick Wood was stripped from him by Mike Johnson, and recovered by Mark Harper on the Pittsburgh 34. The demons came back for a short moment, as Cleveland failed to mount a drive, and Bahr missed a 43-yard field goal attempt on fourth down. Just when things looked bleak, the officials came through to ward off any remaining demons. On Bahr's attempt, Pittsburgh's Dave Edwards ran into Bahr, and was called for roughing the kicker. The penalty gave the Browns possession on the Steelers' 21, and Kosar went to work from there. Throwing to Slaughter and Brian Brennan, Kosar got the Browns to the 4, and from there,

Earnest Byner

Byner ran for a touchdown to give Cleveland a 27-24 lead with eight minutes remaining.

Matt Bahr tried to increase the lead to six points with a 24-yard field goal attempt, but missed. It was the first time in 40 attempts that Bahr missed a field goal from inside 30 yards, and it gave the Steelers a chance to tie or take the lead with 1:38 left.

On a second-and-ten situation from the Cleveland 35, Malone rolled to his left with Earnest Jackson trailing behind him. When defenders rushed in at him, Malone went to pitch the ball to Jackson. Defensive end Sam Clancy got through the line and swatted the ball away from Malone before he could get it to Jackson. Jackson did manage to pick the ball up on a bounce, but Clay Matthews then knocked it free, and Chris Rockins recovered for the Browns on the Cleveland 29. From there, all the Browns did was hold onto the ball for dear life, and at 4:12 pm, the Three Rivers jinx became a thing of the past.

Brian Brennan

Clay Matthews

GREAT BROWNS' VICTORIES OVER PITTSBURGH

November 25, 1973

Trailing 16-14 with two minutes left in the game, Cleveland quarterback Mike Phipps was forced from the pocket near midfield. After avoiding several sack attempts, Phipps saw rookie running back Greg Pruitt all by himself on the Pittsburgh 38. After making the catch, Pruitt electrified the 67,000 plus in attendance by weaving his way through one of the NFL's top defenses for 20 additional yards before being stopped on the 18.

Leroy Kelly

After Leroy Kelly lost a yard on the next play, Pruitt took advantage of excellent blocking and swept the left end. He got around the corner and sprinted into the end zone for the score that put the Browns on top, 21-16, over the division-leading Steelers with one minute remaining. Pittsburgh made it to the Cleveland 15, but four straight incompletions gave the Browns their ninth straight win over Pittsburgh in Municipal Stadium.

October 10, 1976

After three straight losses put them in a 1-3 hole, the Browns' 1976 season looked bleak as they prepared to host the winners of the previous two Super Bowls in week five. The Steelers were also having their problems getting untracked, and shared a 1-3 record with Cleveland.

The game was a hard-hitting affair, which was not uncommon when these two bitter rivals played each other. The hitting was so intense that both teams lost their starting quarterbacks. Brian Sipe suffered a concussion in the first half, and Terry Bradshaw hurt his neck after defensive end Joe Jones lifted him in the air, then threw him down to the turf head first. The Cleveland defense, led by Jones, who tormented Bradshaw and his replacement all day, did a great job holding the explosive Pittsburgh offense in check.

Sipe's replacement was Dave Mays, who entered the game with the Browns down 10-6, but left the game a hero. He called his own plays, completed five of nine passes for 70 yards, and took the Browns to their only touchdown of the game. After Don Cockroft had a 51-yard field goal attempt blocked, the Steelers couldn't get a handle on the loose ball, and Doug Dieken recovered for Cleveland. Dieken's effort helped Mays guide the Browns the rest of the way, and Cleo Miller capped the drive off with the touchdown that put Cleveland in the lead to stay. Cockroft's conversion was wide, but he made up for the miss a

short time later with a 50-yard field goal that gave the Browns a 15-10 advantage going into the fourth quarter.

Mays got Cleveland within field goal range twice in the final quarter. Cockroft missed his first attempt, but hit on a 41-yarder to extend the Browns' lead to 18-10 at the two-minute warning. The Steelers fought back, as back-up quarterback Mike Kruczek threw a 45-yard pass to Lynn Swann, then scored himself on a run from the Cleveland 22. Roy Gerela's conversion was blocked, and the Browns held on for an 18-16 win. This victory helped turn Cleveland's season around, and after two terrible seasons that saw the Browns win a total of seven games, they finished the '76 campaign at 9-5. The Steelers also rebounded, and did even better than the Browns. They went on a ten-game winning streak following this loss, and qualified for the playoff for the

Doug Dieken

fifth straight season. They eventually lost to Oakland in the AFC championship game, but came back two years later to win back-to-back Super Bowls for the second time in their history.

December 18, 1983

In the 1983 season finale, the Browns beat the Steelers, 30-17, in what proved to be Brian Sipe's swan song in a Cleveland uniform. The following season, he jumped over to the USFL, where he finished out his pro career. Sipe might have broken a lot of hearts when he left Cleveland, but he left so many wonderful memories, with one of them coming in his finale.

Sipe played brilliantly against the Steelers, completing 14 of 22 passes for 199 yards and 4 touchdowns. Pittsburgh took an early 3-0 lead, and on the first play following the kickoff, Sipe teamed up with rookie Rocky Belk for a 64-yard touchdown. By halftime, Sipe had two more touchdown passes, a 3-yarder to Harry Holt, and the other from 4 yards to Ricky Feacher, to give the Browns a 23-10 lead.

Sipe almost made an early exit in the third quarter after Pittsburgh's wild man, Jack Lambert, plowed into him on a late hit. Sipe was always tough, and shook the massive blow off, while Lambert was ejected for the flagrant foul. A few plays later, Sipe made the Steelers pay for the hit by

throwing his fourth touchdown pass, and his second of the day to Holt.

On the final play of the game, Franco Harris caught a 2-yard pass from Mark Malone to make the final 30-17.

October 24, 1993

Eric Metcalf was in his fifth season with the Browns, and was one of the most electrifying return men in the league. He was always a threat to score whenever he

Eric Metcalf

touched the ball, and in a home game against the Steelers, he was at his best.

Metcalf had to sit out of practice the week prior to the Steelers' visit to Cleveland in 1993 due to a sprained knee. By Friday he was able to work out, and by Sunday, he was ready to enter the record book.

In the second quarter, with the Browns up 7-0, Metcalf fielded a punt on his 9, and raced 91 yards to the end zone to set a Cleveland record for the longest punt return in team history.

The Steelers tied the game at 14-14 with just seconds left in the half, and were leading, 23-21, with 2:05 remaining in the fourth quarter. The Cleveland defense held, and Mark Royals sent a monstrous 53-yard punt in Metcalf's direction. Metcalf caught the ball on his 25, then sprinted up the right sideline for a touchdown with the entire Pittsburgh special team lagging behind him as he crossed the goal line. With this return, Metcalf entered the NFL record book, as his two punt returns in one game tied a league mark.

Metcalf's exploits had the sold-out stadium rocking, and the Browns held on to win one of the more wilder Pittsburgh-Cleveland games, 28-23. This win over the Steelers was the last time the Browns beat them before moving to Baltimore. At least it was in classic fashion.

BROWNS WIN DIVISIONAL PLAYOFF GAME IN DOUBLE OVERTIME AGAINST THE NEW YORK JETS

[JANUARY 3, 1987]

Frank Minnifield

On January 4, 1986, the Browns blew a 21-3 halftime lead over the heavily favored Miami Dolphins in a divisional playoff game, and lost, 24-21. At the time, Browns backers all over the country were heartsick, but felt that this game might have been a learning experience for the upstart Browns, and that the next season might be the one in which the Super Bowl was finally a reality.

Cleveland did learn from that game, and they came together both offensively and defensively in 1986 to finish atop the Central Division with a 12-4 record, which gave them the most wins of any Browns team since joining the NFL in 1950.

They were led offensively by 23-year-old quarterback Bernie Kosar, who had one of the best football minds in the league at such a young age. In only his first full season at the controls of the offense, Kosar played brilliantly. He completed 310 passes out of 531 attempts for 3,854 yards and 17 touchdowns. He also finished the year with the lowest interception rate in the NFL, throwing only 10. Kevin Mack was the leading ground gainer, and despite missing four games with an injured shoulder, he still managed to run for a team-high 665 yards and 10 touchdowns. Kosar's top receiver was Brian Brennan, who caught 55 passes for 836 yards and six touchdowns. Other key players on offense were receivers Webster Slaughter, Reggie Langhorne, tight end Ozzie Newsome, and running back Earnest Byner, who missed quite a bit of time fighting off injuries after gaining 1,000 yards in 1985.

The defense was one of the top units in the league, boasting four all-pros in Cleveland native Bob Golic, Chip Banks, Hanford Dixon, and Frank Minnifield. Golic anchored the line at nose tackle, Banks led the linebacking corps along with Clay Matthews, and Dixon and Minnifield made up the best cornerback tandem in the NFL.

The New York Jets came into this game after winning a wild card contest over the Kansas City Chiefs. The Jets were coached by Joe Walton, and looked invincible over the first eleven weeks of the season. They were the hottest team in football with a 10-1 record, but then everything came unraveled, and they lost their last five games to just squeak into the playoffs.

The Browns hosted their first playoff game in six years on Saturday, January 3rd. The 78, 106 fans were treated to a sunny day with temperatures in the mid-30s.

The Jets got on the board first with a four-play, 82-yard drive. Quarterback Pat Ryan, who took over as the starting signal caller late in the year, sparked the drive with two big passes. He threw to Al Toon for 28 yards to get the Jets into Cleveland territory, then finished the

quick drive off with a 42-yard touchdown pass to Wesley Walker to give New York a 7-0 lead. With 5:04 left in the first quarter, the Jets looked like the team that was powerful earlier in the season.

Undaunted by the Jets' swift scoring march, Kosar put together one of his own. With 1:44 left in the opening quarter, Kosar took the Browns on a six-play, 98-yard drive. On three of those plays, Kosar found his receivers for big gains. Newsome caught two passes for 44 yards, and Herman Fontenot capped the drive off with a 37-yard reception for the touchdown. Mark Moseley added the extra point to end the first quarter in a 7-7 tie.

The second quarter was not as productive offensively for either team, but they still managed to get points on the board. Cleveland broke the tie when Moseley kicked a 38-yard field goal after Kosar got the Browns within range by completing passes to Newsome for 17 yards and Mack for 25. The Jets tied it back up with two seconds left in the half on a 46-yard field goal by Pat Leahy.

Kosar had trouble moving the Browns throughout the third quarter, and New York couldn't do much better, but they did get a 37-yard field goal out of Leahy to go into the fourth quarter leading, 13-10.

Kosar finally got the offense going, and got to the New York 2-yard line. On third down, he tried to force a pass to Slaughter, who was double-teamed in the end zone. The result was Kosar's first interception in 133 straight attempts, and it was Russell Carter who ended the streak in the corner of the end zone.

The Cleveland defense forced the Jets to punt, and Kosar took over on his 17. Once again, Kosar suffered an inter-

Cleveland defensemen
Hanford Dixon, Chip Banks
and Bob Golic (clockwise,
from top).

Reggie Langhorne

ception on the first play of the drive. This time it was Jerry Holmes who picked the ball off, and he gave the Jets great field position on the Browns' 25.

New York made short order of the Browns, as Freeman McNeil took a handoff on first down, and after bouncing off several defenders, ran to the outside and scored easily. Leahy's conversion put the Jets up 20-10 with 4:14 left in regulation. A large number of fans had seen enough, and started to head for the exits with disgusted looks on their faces.

Some of the fans might have given up, but Kosar hadn't, and as he entered the huddle on Cleveland's next possession, he told his teammates that they were going to win. Not bad leadership for a 23 year old in his first complete season. Talk is cheap, but Kosar followed up his words by throwing five straight completions during this drive. Cleveland was aided on this drive by an overexcited Mark Gastineau.

Gastineau began taunting some fans while standing behind the bench after New York went up by ten points. He was an emotional player who was pumped up all the time during a game, and after taunting the fans, he went onto the field to harass the Browns for the final four minutes. On the first play of the drive, Gastineau roughed up Kosar after he

Webster Slaughter

The game looked to be in the hands of the Jets, but Cleveland refused to give in, and played inspired football. They knocked the Jets back three yards in three plays and forced them to punt.

Kosar took over possession on his 33 with 51 ticks left in regulation. The Jets once again hurt themselves with another major penalty, this one being a pass interference call that moved the Browns into New York territory at the 42. Slaughter then made a fantastic catch off a defender's helmet at the 5 to give Moseley a chance at the tying field goal. The 13-year veteran who came to Cleveland after Matt Bahr got injured, made the Browns glad they had him when his 22-yard field goal sent the game into overtime tied at 20-20.

The Jets won the overtime coin toss, but got nowhere. Kosar then took over on his 26, and moved the Browns to the New York 5 after hitting Langhorne with a 35-yard pass. Moseley came in to end it, but he was off balance in his approach, and barely got his foot on the ball. The sloppy kick went wide, and the Jets had new life.

New York was unable to gather any momentum from Moseley's miss, and gave the ball back over to the Browns with 2:38 left in the first overtime period.

Cleveland began on their 31, and were facing a fatigued New York defense. Kosar decided to attack the weakened line

threw an incompletion, with the result being a penalty that gave the Browns the ball on their 33.

It was then that Kosar hit on those five passes in a row. He threw two each to Langhorne and Brennan, and one to running back Curtis Dickey that got Cleveland to the New York 1 at the two-minute warning. When play was resumed, Mack scored and Moseley kicked the extra point to make it 20-17 with 1:57 left.

Moseley tried an onside kick, but New York recovered on the Cleveland 45.

by sending Mack on power runs up the middle. The strategy worked, as Mack pounded his way for a first down at the Cleveland 41. He then slammed into the line for another eight yards to get the Browns to midfield two plays later. Mack seemed to be getting stronger with each run while the Jets were sucking for air. Mack carried three straight times for a total of 26 yards to get the Browns to the New York 9, and to give Moseley another chance at winning it.

The Jets called timeout to make Moseley think about the pressure riding on him, but he was a veteran kicker focused on the job at hand. He was mad at himself for his earlier mishap, and wanted a chance at redemption.

Kicking toward the Dawg Pound with the entire crowd on their feet shouting, Moseley calmly set himself up, and split the uprights with a perfect 27-yard kick to make the Browns victors in the playoffs for the first time since 1969, with two minutes expired from the clock in the second overtime period.

When this classic 23-20 Cleveland victory finally ended, it was the third

Mark Moseley

longest in NFL history, and 17 new play-off records were set. The brilliant play of Bernie Kosar accounted for three of those records, as he set them for most completions (33), most attempts (64), and most passing yards (489).

The excitement over this team equaled that of the Kardiac Kids days, and the Browns had the whole city of Cleveland on such a high for a week. Everywhere you looked, people were clad in Browns merchandise, and songs were played on the radio about the team. The entire city of Cleveland was pained orange and brown in anticipation of a Super Bowl bid.

Unfortunately, like so many times in Cleveland sports history, something happens to suck the life right out of the town's sports fans. This time it was what came to be known as "The Drive", and it was conducted by Denver quarterback John Elway, who is at the top of the Cleveland sports fan's top ten hate list. Elway led his team to a late score that sent the game into overtime. He then proceeded to get them close enough for the game-winning field goal to kill the Browns' Super Bowl bid by the score of 23-20.

BROWNS DEFEAT SUPER BOWL CHAMPION DALLAS COWBOYS TO CLINCH PLAYOFF SPOT

[DECEMBER 10, 1994]

Dallas came into the 1994 season as winners of the previous two Super Bowls, and were well on their way to going for a third when Cleveland came to Texas Stadium on December 10th with hopes of making the playoffs for the first time since 1989.

In the late 1980s, the Browns were one of the NFL's elite. They made it to the AFC championship game following the 1986, 87, and 89 seasons, but lost out on Super Bowl bids each time to the Denver Broncos. By 1990, the team was in shambles, as they recorded a 3-13 record, which tied them with the 1975 team for the worst in club history. Head coach Bud Carson, who took over after Marty Schottenheimer left following the 1988 season, was fired midway through the season.

In 1991, Art Modell hired his eighth head coach in former New York Giants assistant, Bill Belichick. Belichick improved the team to 6-10 the following year, then had back-to-back 7-9 seasons. By 1994, he seemed to be going in the right direction, and took his team into Dallas with a 9-4 record.

Bill Belichick

The Cowboys were heavy ten-and-a-half point favorites to beat the upstart Browns, and jumped out to a 7-0 lead late in the first quarter. Quarterback Troy Aikman had missed the two previous games due to a knee injury, and was shaky from the start. He quickly got back in the groove, and led Dallas to the game's first score. Emmitt Smith helped by running for 26 yards on one play, then caught a 7-yard touchdown pass from Aikman.

Cleveland didn't seemed to be intimidated by the Dallas mystic, and put together an impressive drive of their own against one of the NFL's top rated defenses. Aided by a 48-yard pass interference penalty that put the ball on the Dallas 9, Vinny Testaverde threw a 2-yard touchdown pass to Michael Jackson with no time left on the clock in the first quarter. Matt Stover's conversion tied it at 7-7.

The Browns took a 10-7 lead on a Stover 34-yard field goal late in the second quarter. The field goal was set up when Alvin Harper fumbled, and Stevon Moore recovered for Cleveland on the Dallas 47. Eight plays later, Stover gave the Browns the lead at halftime.

Vinny Testaverde

Stover increased Cleveland's lead to 13-7 at start of fourth quarter with a 32-yard field goal. A minute-and-a-half later, he hit on his fourth field goal of the day, this time from 43 yards. That three-pointer was set up when Don Griffin intercepted Aikman at the Dallas 45. Testaverde got the Browns closer with a 16-yard pass to Jackson, then it was Stover who booted the Cleveland's sixteenth point of the game.

With 6:21 left in the game, Dallas closed the gap to 16-14 with a 12-play, 78-yard drive. Smith was the workhorse for the Cowboys on this drive, as he carried on eight of the twelve plays for 39 yards, with the final one going for a touchdown from the 4.

The Browns stalled on their next possession, and pinned the Cowboys deep on their own 8 following the punt on fourth down. With time running out, the Cowboys were faced with a fourth down situation on their 16, but fumbled right into the hands of Bill Johnson. Cleveland couldn't get into the end zone, but Stover did increase the Cleveland lead to 19-14 with a 32-yard field goal.

With 1:49 left, Stover's fifth field goal forced the Cowboys to score a touchdown to win, and they almost pulled it out. Kevin Williams had a beautiful 42-yard kickoff return that set the Cowboys up in good shape on their 49. With 23 seconds left, Aikman completed a pass to Williams for 15 yards over the middle to the Cleveland 6. Aikman then grounded the ball to stop the clock. The following play was the final one, and Aikman threw to tight end Jay Novacek. Hard-hitting Eric Turner shook off the pain of an injured shoulder to stop Novacek six inches from the goal line to preserve the upset victory.

Cleveland clinched a playoff berth with the win, and finished the season at 11-5. They beat the New England Patriots in a wild card contest, then were completely dominated by the Pittsburgh Steelers in the next round, 29-9.

The Cowboys rebounded from the surprise loss to the Browns, and won the NFC Eastern Division with a record of 12-4. They whipped Green Bay in their first playoff game, but the quest for a third straight Super Bowl victory ended the following weekend with a 38-28 loss to San Francisco in the NFC championship game.

Eric Turner (29)

BROWNS TIMELINE

[1995–1999]

The following section consists of a timeline from the Browns' move to Baltimore in November, 1995, until their return to the field in August, 1999:

1995

November 5

Browns owner Art Modell shocks the city of Cleveland with the announcement that he will move the team to Baltimore, Maryland after the 1995 season is over. At the time of the announcement, the Browns were 4-5 in the AFC Central Division, and tied with Houston for second place behind Pittsburgh.

December 17

In the final home game ever played in Cleveland Municipal Stadium, the Browns snap a six-game losing streak with a 26-10 win over Cincinnati. This marked the first time the Browns won a game since Modell's plans to move.

December 24

In their last game of the turbulent '95 campaign, the Browns lose to the expansion Jacksonville Jaguars down in Florida, 24-21, to end their final year in Cleveland under Modell's ownership at 5-11. It proved to be their worst finish in six seasons.

1996

February 8

Art Modell gets the official announcement from the other 29 NFL owners that his move to Baltimore can proceed. In the deal, Modell had to pay the city of Cleveland $11.5 million. The NFL office also agreed to grant Cleveland a new team in 1999 if the city built a new stadium. To get things going, the NFL loaned the city of Cleveland $48 million for the new facility.

April 23

City officials come to an agreement that the new stadium will be built on the exact location as Cleveland Municipal Stadium.

April 25

For $350,000 a year, the NFL rents out the Browns headquarters in Berea, Ohio.

June 26

Bill Futterer is put in charge of the Cleveland Browns Trust Fund by the NFL.

September 21-22

Over the course of these two days, over 65,000 people get a chance to walk through Cleveland Municipal Stadium before demolition on it begins in November, 1996.

November 25

At 9:00 a.m., the wrecking ball swung its initial punch at Municipal Stadium in the bleacher section. Many were on hand to see their memories of the 65-year old structure begin to crumble. Within two months, the stadium was completely gone.

1997

May 15

A ground-breaking ceremony officially kicked off the start of construction on the new stadium, which was projected at the time to cost nearly $250 million.

October 12

Football fever begins to sweep the city, as close to 53,000 applications for tickets come through the Browns offices.

1998

January 16

Real Estate developer Bart Wolstein is the first to announce his interest in owning the new Cleveland Browns. A native Clevelander, Wolstein's team also included former star Browns' players, Mike McCormack and Dick Schafrath.

March 3

With much-awaited anticipation, a scale model of the new 72,000 seat stadium is unveiled at Cleveland City Hall, and was on display for public viewing until the end of March.

March 23

The National Football League put an end to speculation regarding what existing franchise might be coming to Cleveland with the announcement that the new Browns were going to an expansion team that would begin play in August, 1999.

March 25

Thomas Murdough, founder of Little Tikes Toy Company and Step 2, became the second person to express interest in owning the Browns.

1998 (CONTD.)

April 8

The list of potential owners continues to grow as cable television moguls, Charles and Larry Dolan announces their desire to purchase the Browns. By the middle of June, actor Bill Cosby and former Miami Dolphins head coach Don Shula join their team. Shula was also a native Clevelander who played for the Browns from 1951 to 53 before going on to become the winningest pro football coach in history.

May 15

New York businessman Howard Milstein becomes the fourth to express interest in buying the Cleveland franchise. He is joined in his quest by former Browns Calvin Hill and Paul Warfield, along with six top Cleveland-based corporate executives from various companies.

July 7

Cleveland Indians owner Richard Jacobs announces his interest in buying the Browns after helping guide the Indians to two World Series appearances in 1995 and '97.

July 23

Al Lerner, chairman and chief executive officer of MBNA, one of the country's largest credit card companies, announces his plans to pursue ownership of the Cleveland Browns. Born in Brooklyn, New York, Lerner has been a resident of the Cleveland area for 40 years. Also included on Lerner's team are beloved ex-Browns' quarterback Bernie Kosar, and Carmen Policy.

Bernie Kosar

1998 (CONTD.)

After serving in the San Francisco 49ers front office for fifteen years, former Youngstown, Ohio native Policy resigned a day before Lerner's announced plans to buy the Browns. In his days as an executive with the 49ers, Policy was instrumental in guiding the team to four Super Bowl championships. Throughout football circles, Policy is regarded as a master of the salary cap, and at obtaining tremendous talent through the free agent market. He was honored by *The Sporting News* and *Pro Football Weekly*, was the 1994 NFL Executive of the Year, which was the same year that the 49ers won their fifth Super Bowl since 1981.

August 17

Jeremy Jacobs, owner of the Boston Bruins hockey team, announces his interest in purchasing the Browns.

August 31

After joining forces to make a stronger bid to buy the Browns, Thomas Murdough and Richard Jacobs bow out of the race for ownership. Jeremy Jacobs also ends his pursuit of the team.

September 8

Al Lerner wins in the race to purchase the new Cleveland Browns with a 29-0-1 vote from the other NFL owners. He also set a new record by dishing out $530 million to buy the Browns, which is the largest amount ever paid for a professional sports franchise. The second-place finishers in the race to buy the Browns were the Dolan group, who made a bid of $500 million.

November 30

The Browns announce the hiring of Dwight Clark as vice president and director of football operations. Prior to coming to Cleveland, Clark had made a name for himself in the San Francisco 49ers' organization as both a player and executive.

After a college career at Clemson University, Clark became the 10th-round draft pick of the 49ers in 1979. In a pro career that had many great moments, the greatest was his game-winning catch of a Joe Montana pass in the NFC Championship game following the 1981 season. Clark's spectacular catch with seconds remaining clinched the team's first trip to the Super Bowl, which they won over Cincinnati, 26-21.

After the 1987 season, Clark retired from the playing field as the 49ers all-time reception leader with 506 catches. With those catches he gained 6,750 yards, and caught 48 touchdowns. Clark then went into the 49ers' front office. He started out in the marketing department in 1989, and by the mid-90s, he was serving the team as its director of football operations. At the time of his leaving the team to come to Cleveland, Clark was the 49ers' executive vice president during the 1998 season.

December 22

Six players are signed as free agents, thus becoming the first members of the new Cleveland Browns. They are linebacker Darion Conner, defensive tackles Albert Reese and Bill Duff, defensive back Corey Dowden, quarterback John Dutton, and receiver Corey Bridges.

December 23

Added three more players to the roster with the free agent signings of tight end Aaron Laing, defensive tackle Chris Maumalanga, and special team performer John Henry Mills.

December 28

Started off the hunt for a head coach by interviewing Brian Billick, who was the offensive coordinator for the Minnesota Vikings. Under Billick, the 1998 Vikings offense was virtually unstoppable throughout the 1998 season.

December 29

The Browns interview another top offensive coordinator. This time it is Gary Kubiak of the Denver Broncos, who were gearing up to repeat as Super Bowl champions during Kubiak's interview.

1999

January 8

The Browns expand their roster to 14 players by signing offensive linemen Hicham El-Mashtoub and Steve Zahursky, linebacker Randy Neal, wide receiver Jermaine Ross, and running back Pepe Pearson, who was a local high school star from Euclid, Ohio, and later at Ohio State University.

January 18

Brian Billick's name is taken off the Browns' list of possible head coaching candidates. Billick decided that he was more interested in the head coaching job with Art Modell's Baltimore Ravens, and signed on as their new coach on January 19th.

Denver's Gary Kubiak also announces that he is no longer interested in pursuing the head coaching job in Cleveland, and has decided to stay with the Broncos as their offensive coordinator.

January 19

The Oakland Raiders' defensive coordinator, Willie Shaw, meets with Carmen Policy regarding the still-vacant head coaching job.

January 21

After two interviews, the Cleveland Browns announced that Chris Palmer would become the 11th head coach in team history. The 49-year old Palmer came to the Browns after serving as the Jacksonville Jaguars' offensive coordinator in 1997 and 98. He was credited with the success of the Jaguars' star quarterback Mark Brunell, as well as other high-profile signal callers throughout his coaching career such as Doug Flutie and Drew Bledsoe.

Prior to his time in Jacksonville, Palmer played quarterback at Southern Connecticut State. After serving as an assistant at the University of Connecticut, Lehigh, and Colgate, Palmer became the head coach at the University of New Haven in 1986. After two seasons there, he took over the head job at Boston University from 1988 to '89.

Palmer moved on to the professional ranks following his stay at Boston University, and took his first pro job in the Canadian Football League as the offensive line coach for the Montreal Concordes in 1983. The next two seasons were spent as the receivers coach, and then offensive coordinator, for the New Jersey Generals of the United States Football League. While with the Generals, Palmer had the opportunity to work with the leader of the Kardiac Kids, Brian Sipe, who signed on as quarterback with New Jersey after leaving the Browns after the 1983 season. Palmer eventually came to the NFL in 1990 as the receivers coach with the Houston Oilers. In 1993, he went to work for Bill Parcells in New England. During his stay with the Patriots, Palmer served as Parcells' receivers coach, then quarterback coach. It was under Palmer's coaching that New England quarterback Drew Bledsoe emerged as one of the NFL's top signal callers. Palmer's great effort with Bledsoe was one of the reasons the Patriots were AFC champions in 1996. After the Super Bowl season of 1996, Palmer left the Patriots to become Jacksonville's offensive coordinator under head coach Tom Coughlin.

January 25

Chris Palmer names Bob Slowik as his defensive coordinator, and Clarence Brooks as defensive line coach.

January 27

Palmer announces that Bob Pelcic will be his offensive line coach.

January 30

The Browns' legendary tight end Ozzie Newsome gets word that he had been elected into the Pro Football Hall of Fame along with Lawrence Taylor, Eric Dickerson, Billy Shaw, and former Cleveland native Tom Mack.

February 2

Billy Davis is named defensive quality-control coach. Tony Sparano is named offensive quality-control coach. Keith Kidd is named pro personnel director.

1999 (CONTD.)

February 4

Jerry Holmes is named defensive backfield coach. Dick Portee is named offensive backfield coach.

February 5

John Hufnagel is named quarterback coach. Ken Whisenhunt is named special teams coach.

February 8

Ray Perkins is named tight end coach. Tim Jorgensen is named strength coach.

February 9

In Canton, Ohio, the Browns select 37 players in the expansion draft. Center-guard Jim Pyne makes history by being selected number one by the Browns. After five years with the Detroit Lions, the 27-year-old Pyne started all 16 regular season games at center for the Lions in 1998. Both his grandfather and father also played pro football.

February 11

Jerry Butler is named receivers coach. Mark Michaels is named quality-control coach for special teams.

February 16

Cleveland signs two more free agents, offensive tackle Orlando Brown and cornerback Corey Fuller. Also coming to Cleveland was middle linebacker Chris Spielman, who the Browns received in a trade with Buffalo for past considerations. Spielman is a hard-hitting linebacker with an incredible work ethic from Massillon, Ohio, and later Ohio State University.

1999 (CONTD.)

February 22

The Browns trade their fourth- and fifth-round picks of the 1998 college draft to San Francisco in exchange for quarterback Ty Detmer, who signs a seven-year deal with the Browns.

February 25

Defensive end John Thierry, formally of the Chicago Bears, signs a one-year contract with the Browns.

March 1

The Arizona Cardinals' offensive tackle Lomas Brown agrees to come to Cleveland. Two days later, both parties make it official when Brown signs a three-year contract.

March 4

Running back Terry Kirby signs a two-year contract with Cleveland after last playing with the San Francisco 49ers.

March 26 -28

For the first time in four years, the Cleveland Browns take to the practice field at the Browns complex in Berea for a weekend mini-camp that consists of 73 players.

April 17

With the first pick in the 1999 college draft, the Cleveland Browns select quarterback Tim Couch from the University of Kentucky. After announcing his decision in January to bypass his senior season and enter the NFL draft, Couch becomes one of the college players most sought after by the Browns. The other top candidates were Oregon quarterback Akili Smith, and 1998 Heisman Trophy winning running back Ricky Williams out of Texas.

1999 (CONTD.)

The 6-4, 220-pound Couch became the 19th quarterback selected number one overall since 1944, and appears to have all the tools needed to be a top-notch signal caller and team leader. He was a finalist in the 1998 Heisman Trophy voting, and appears to have all the makings of a talented quarterback. With a coach like Chris Palmer, who has a knack at grooming quarterbacks, behind him, the future looks bright for Tim Couch.

A native of Hyden, Kentucky, Couch established himself as one of the most sought after quarterbacks ever.

Tim Couch, right, with Cleveland Browns owner Al Lerner after the Browns made him the number-one pick overall in the 1999 NFL draft.

He decided to stay in his home state, and became a starter for the University of Kentucky in his freshman season. In 1998, Couch averaged 388 passing yards per game. He completed 400 out of 553 passes for 4,275 yards, and 36 touchdowns.

Here's a look at Cleveland's other draft picks
for 1999 in the order they were selected by the Browns:

Kevin Johnson

5-10, 188-pound wide receiver from Syracuse. Johnson was an All-American kick returner, and was honored by being named the Big East Special Teams Player of the Year in 1998. He set a Syracuse record by catching 60 passes for 894 yards and nine touchdowns in 1998.

He was selected in the second round by the Browns, and was the 32nd over-all pick.

Rahim Abdullah

6-5, 244-pound linebacker from Clemson. Abdullah earned first-team All-Atlantic Coast Conference honors in 1998. He was selected in the second round, and was the 45th overall pick.

Daylon McCutcheon

5-8, 180-pound defensive back from Southern Cal. McCutcheon was an All-Pac 10 first-team selection, and third-team All-American. He was selected in the third round, and was the 62nd overall pick.

Marquis Smith

6-2, 213-pound safety from the University of California. Regarded as one of the hardest-hitting defensive backs in the nation, Smith earned first-team All-Pac

10 honors in 1998. Smith was selected in the third round, and was the 76th overall pick.

Wali Ranier

6-2, 235-pound linebacker from the University of Virginia. Regarded as a very intense player, Ranier led Virginia with 134 tackles. He also had five sacks, and two interceptions. He was an All-Atlantic Coast Conference first-team selection, and third-team All-American. He was selected in the fourth round, and was the 124th overall pick.

Darrin Chiaverini

6-1, 205-pound wide receiver from the University of Colorado. Chiaverini is regarded as a position receiver who comes up with the tough catches. He has a strong work ethic, and these qualities helped him earn a place on the All-Big 12 second-team. During the 1998 season, Chiaverini caught 52 passes for 630 yards and five touchdowns. He was selected in the fifth round, and was the 148th overall pick.

Marcus Spriggs

6-4, 314-pound defensive tackle from Troy (Alabama) State. Spriggs earned a spot on the All-Southland Football League first-team. He also served as team captain in 1998. He was selected in the sixth round, and was the 174th overall pick.

Kendall Ogle

6-0, 230-pound linebacker from the University of Maryland. Ogle was Maryland's team captain in 1998, and was honorable mention All-Atlantic Coast Conference. He registered 143 tackles, which gave him a second-place finish in that category in the conference. He has great speed, and is a very tough tackler. He was selected in the sixth round, and was the 187th overall pick.

1999 DRAFT PICKS (CONTD.)

James Dearth

6-3, 269-pound tight end from Tarleton State in Texas. Dearth earned first-team All-Lone Star Conference honors, and won the Most Valuable Lineman award. He is a big, strong player who blocks extremely well. Dearth was selected in the sixth round, and was the 191st overall pick.

Madres Hill

5-11, 200-pound running back from the University of Arkansas. After an incredible sophomore season, in which he gained 1,387 yards, Hill suffered knee injuries over the course of his junior and senior seasons. He seemed to regain some of his brilliance during the 1998 season, and managed to rush for 669 yards. If his knees can hold up, look for Hill to be a breakaway threat. He was selected in the seventh round, and was the 207th overall pick.

BROWNS IN THE HALL OF FAME

This section is dedicated to the 14 members of the Cleveland Browns' proud heritage that have been honored with induction into the Pro Football Hall of Fame in Canton, Ohio.

Otto Graham
Class of 1965

While at Northwestern University, Graham was a gifted all-around athlete. In football he was a standout tailback, but when Paul Brown saw him, he had visions of making him a quarterback. After becoming the Browns' first-ever draft pick, it was at quarterback that Graham wound up, and over the course of ten seasons, he not only played the position, but became a master of it.

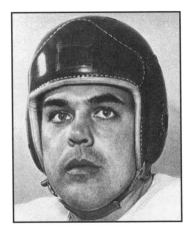

Otto Graham

Graham led the Browns to championship game appearances in each of his ten seasons, which is a mark that will never be equaled or broken. Along the way, he won seven league championships, four Most Valuable Player awards, four passing percentage titles, and earned a spot on the all-pro team every year he played. He ended his brilliant career with 23,584 yards passing, and 174 touchdowns. He became the first member of the Cleveland Browns to be inducted into the hall of fame. His number 14 was retired by the Cleveland organization.

Paul Brown
Class of 1967

When you think of Paul Brown, you think of football. Almost everything one sees in football today can be traced back to him. Brown started using full-time coaching staffs, developed intelligence tests for his players, made use of game films to grade their performances, made classroom studies commonplace, issued each man a playbook for studying when not at practice, and much more. He was one of the best judges of talents the game has ever known, and drilled his players until they could execute a play to perfection. These are just a few of the many things that Brown brought to the game.

Paul Brown

He was a winner in every stage of his coaching career. After creating a dynasty at Massillon High School, he led Ohio State to a national championship in 1942. While in the Navy, he built the Great Lakes Naval Training Station team into a huge success.

When it was time for him to take the next step, which was into the professional ranks, not many people were surprised when Paul Brown produced winner after winner. In his 17 seasons as coach of the Browns, he posted a 167-53-8 record, 11 trips to the championship game, and seven league crowns.

After being fired from the Browns in 1963, he turned up in Cincinnati five years later, and built the Bengals into a solid football team. He coached the team from 1968 through 75, then went into the front office as general manager. From that position, Brown was responsible for the Bengals making two trips to the Super Bowl in the 1980s. Paul Brown died on August 5, 1991 at the age of 82.

Marion Motley
Class of 1968

Anytime the expression power back is used, Marion Motley's name has to come to mind.

At 6-1, 240 pounds, Motley had power and speed, which made for a deadly combination against enemy defenses. He is also regarded as the best blocking back to ever play.

One of the main reasons for Cleveland's success in their early years was a balanced offense. Graham took care of the passing, and Motley the running. A play the Browns made famous during this time was the "trap", in which Graham looked like he was going to throw, and once the defense was sucked in, he handed off to Motley, who ran straight ahead, usually with devastating results.

Motley played for the Browns from 1946 to 1953, and Pittsburgh in 1955. He ran for 4,712 yards, 39 touchdowns and a 5.7 yards per carry average. He led the NFL in rushing with 810 yards in 1950. He died on June 27, 1999.

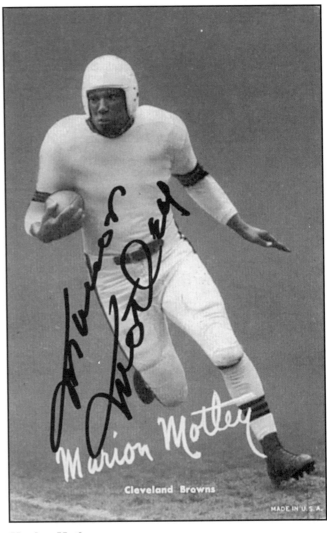

Marion Motley

Jim Brown
Class of 1971

So much has already been said about Jim Brown in this book, but there is still more to say. In his nine seasons, Brown led the league in rushing eight times, was selected all-pro eight times, went to the Pro Bowl after each of his nine seasons, winning the MVP award after the 1966 contest, which proved to be his final game. He also won three NFL Most Valuable Player award in 1958, 1963, and 1965. While filming the movie "The Dirty Dozen" in England prior to the 1966 season, Brown announced his retirement, much to the amazement of the football world. He was still at the top of his game, and never suffered any major injuries considering all the pounding he took from defenses that were geared up to stop him.

Jim Brown walked away from the game like so many wish they could, still in his prime, and still a winner. There is no telling how much yardage Brown could have racked up if he stayed in the game, but one can only guess when pondering that question. What is known is that Brown left the game as its all-time leading rusher with 12,312 yards, and a record 106 touchdowns. He also caught 262 passes for an additional 2,499 yards and 20 touchdowns. His name appeared under virtually every rushing statistic in the NFL record at the time of his retirement, and he still remains the greatest runner to ever carry a football. Needless to say, his number 32 was retired by the Cleveland organization.

Jim Brown

Lou Groza
Class of 1974

Lou Groza's retirement in 1968 brought down the final curtain on the Browns' dynasty years. He was the last member of the original Browns player from 1946 to retire, and did so after 21 seasons. At the time of his retirement, Groza was the NFL's all-time leading scorer with 1,608 points. During his time as Cleveland's kicker, Groza won many games in the closing moments, and twice led the league in scoring.

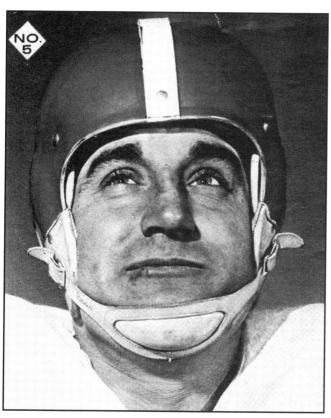

Lou Groza

With so much emphasis placed on his kicking prowess, Groza's abilities as an offensive tackle seem to be all but forgotten. The truth is that he was one of the best tackles of his time, playing the position from 1946 to 1959. During that time span, Groza earned eight spots on the all-pro team, played in eight Pro Bowls, and won *The Sporting News* MVP award in 1954. A back injury forced him to miss the 1960 season, but Groza returned the following year at the age of 37 strictly as a kicker. He is also the only player to ever be on all eight of Cleveland's championship teams.

Dante Lavelli
Class of 1975

Lavelli was Graham's favorite target for their ten seasons together in Cleveland. He was nicknamed "Glue Fingers", because he virtually caught everything thrown his way.

Lavelli was a quarterback in high school, but switched to end at Paul Brown's request while at Ohio State. Brown's keen evaluation of talent made Lavelli a star, and helped earn him all-pro honors in each of his four AAFC seasons, as well as twice in the NFL. He was also named to three Pro Bowls. In 11 seasons with the Browns, Lavelli had 386 receptions for 6,488 yards and 62 touchdowns.

Len Ford
Class of 1976

Len Ford was inducted into the hall of fame posthumously, having died much too early at age 46 of a heart condition in 1972. He will never be forgotten, however, due to his incredible football prowess. Ford was a fast and powerful 6-5, 260-pound defensive end who earned a reputation as the most feared pass rusher of his time.

After earning All-American honors at the University of Michigan, Ford played two seasons with the AAFC's Los Angeles Dons in 1948-49 before coming to the Browns. His career in Cleveland lasted from 1950 through 57, and during his stay, Ford was selected all-pro four times, and played in four Pro Bowls. He finished out his playing career with the Green Bay Packers in 1958.

Bill Willis
Class of 1977

Willis was a member of the original Browns in 1946, and played with them as a middle guard until retiring after the 1953 season. Over those eight seasons as the anchor of the defensive line, Willis was a devastating tackler with exceptional quickness. He was rewarded for his play by being named all-pro seven times, and selected to three Pro Bowls.

Bobby Mitchell
Class of 1983

When he retired after the 1968 season, Bobby Mitchell ranked third all-time in total yards gained with 14, 078. His 91 touchdowns were good enough to earn him fifth place all-time in that category.

Bobby Mitchell

Mitchell came to the Browns in 1958 after a splendid career at the University of Illinois. He was the complete offensive package, excelling at running the ball, catching it, and returning kickoffs and punts. With Olympic speed, Mitchell was a threat to score whenever the ball was in his hands.

In 1962, Mitchell was traded to the Washington Redskins, and that is where he really blossomed into a hall of famer. In his first season in Washington, Mitchell led the league in receptions (72), and receiving yards (1,384). Over his first six seasons with the Redskins, he averaged 63 catches a year. He was named all-pro twice, and played in four Pro Bowls throughout 11 seasons.

Paul Warfield
Class of 1983

Warfield was Cleveland's number-one draft pick in 1964, and made an immediate impact on the team as a wide receiver. His team-leading 52 receptions for 920 yards and nine touchdowns helped the Browns on their way to the 1964 NFL championship. He was blessed with speed that made him a deep threat, and was also one of the most graceful receivers to ever play the game. He made catching a football look effortless, and was one of the most popular players in Cleveland from 1964 to 1969.

In quite possibly the worst trade ever made by the Browns, Warfield was sent to the Miami Dolphins in 1970 for the rights to the first draft pick. While Cleveland got Purdue quarterback Mike Phipps for seven subpar seasons, the Dolphins got a player who helped them get to three straight Super Bowls. The Dolphins won two world championships (1972-73), with the '72 team going undefeated with Warfield as one of the starting receivers.

After leaving Miami following the 1974 season, Warfield played for the Memphis Southmen of the World Football League in 1975. He then returned to Cleveland in 1976 for his two final seasons. He caught 427 passes throughout his career, for 8,565 yards and 85 touchdowns. Warfield had an amazing 20.1 yards per catch average, and caught a touchdown pass in one out of every five receptions.

Mike McCormack
Class of 1984

Paul Brown was so impressed with 6-4, 245-pound offensive tackle Mike McCormack, that he traded 10 players to Baltimore in exchange for five, just to

Paul Warfield

get him. Brown only saw McCormack play during the exhibition season while with the New York Yanks in 1951, but he liked the potential in the young man.

After two years in the military, McCormack came to the Browns in 1954, and showed once again that Paul Brown had no equal when it came to judging talent. McCormack quickly became the leader of the offensive line from his right tackle spot, and was elected team captain in 1956, and served in that capacity until his retirement following the 1962 season. He was responsible for opening many of the holes that Jim Brown ran through early in the runner's career, and also was an excellent pass blocker. He played in three NFL title games with the Browns, and six Pro Bowls.

Frank Gatski
Class of 1985:

Nicknamed "Gunner", Gatski could also have been called "Collector of Championship Rings". In his 12 seasons of pro football, the 6-3, 240-pound center played in 11 league championship games, winning eight of them. He won seven with Cleveland, and one with Detroit in 1957.

Gatski was as outstanding a center as there ever was. He had size, toughness, and strength. He was capable of holding his own against anyone facing him, and was very hard to move. He also had durability. In his 12 seasons, Gatski never missed a practice or a game. It was this strong work ethic that made him a four-time all-pro and hall of famer.

Frank Gatski

Leroy Kelly
Class of 1994:

Kelly was Cleveland's eighth-round draft pick in 1964, and in his first two seasons, he carried the ball only 43 times. This was due to the fact that Kelly played behind the great Jim Brown. While waiting for his chance at becoming a starting running back some day, Kelly established himself as one of the top return men of the mid-sixties, and in 1965 he was the number-one ranked punt returner in the league.

Upon Jim Brown's retirement, Kelly took over the legendary runner's spot in the backfield. It didn't take him long to prove that he was capable of filling the

Leroy Kelly

huge void created by Brown's retirement. In his first season as a starter, Kelly ran for 1,141 yards, and a league-leading 15 touchdowns. In his next two seasons, there was no better running back in the NFL. In 1967, Kelly led the league with 1,205 yards, and in 1968, he topped it again with 1,239 yards. He also led the league in rushing touchdowns both of those seasons.

Kelly was exceptionally quick off the ball, had great balance, and only missed four games over the course of ten seasons with the Browns. He was at his best when running between the tackles, and was one of the best muddy field runners in the history of the game.

When Leroy Kelly retired in 1974, his 7,274 rushing yards ranked him fourth all-time, and his 12,239 total yards also put him near the top in that category as well. He was an all-pro selection five times, and played in six Pro Bowls.

Ozzie Newsome
Class of 1999:

The legendary University of Alabama football coach Bear Bryant once said that Ozzie Newsome was the best end he ever coached. Not bad coming from a man who retired as the winningest college coach in history.

It didn't take Newsome long to show why Bryant was right in making such a statement once he was drafted in the first round by the Browns in 1978. He became the first rookie in 25 years to win the Cleveland TD Club's Offensive MVP award after catching 38 passes for 589 yards and two touchdowns. He also ran the reverse around end 13 times for 96 yards and two touchdowns. He was only held catchless one time during his rookie season, and made the all-rookie team.

Ozzie Newsome

From then on Newsome became one of the premier receivers in the NFL, and by the time he retired in 1991, his name was right up at the top of the list among the elite pass catchers in history. He caught 662 passes, which ranked him fourth all-time in the NFL, and number one on the Browns. He gained 7,980 yards, scored 47 touchdowns, and caught at least one pass in 150 straight games. He had great hands, and only fumbled a few times in his career. Newsome also became the tenth NFL player in history to have 50 or more receptions in six seasons. He was a seven time all-pro, and played in three Pro Bowls.

CLEVELAND BROWNS STATISTICS AND HONORS

BROWNS SEASON RECORDS (1946—1995)

1946 to 1949—played in All-America Football Conference
1950 to 1995—played in National Football League

1946

12-2—finished first in AAFC Western Division. Won AAFC championship game, 14-9, against New York Yankees.

1947

12-1-1—finished first in AAFC Western Division. Won AAFC championship game, 14-3, against New York Yankees.

1948

14-0—finished first in AAFC Western Division. Won AAFC championship game, 49-7, against Buffalo Bills.

1949

9-1-2—Defeated Buffalo Bills in divisional playoff, 31-21. Won AAFC championship game, 21-7, against San Francisco 49ers.

1950

10-2—Tied New York Giants for American Conference title. Defeated Giants in special playoff, 8-3, to advance to NFL championship game. Won NFL championship game, 30-28, against Los Angeles Rams.

1951

11-1—finished first in American Conference. Lost to Los Angeles Rams in NFL championship game, 24-17.

1952

8-4—finished first in American Conference. Lost to Detroit Lions in NFL championship game, 17-7.

1953

11-1—finished first in Eastern Conference. Lost to Detroit Lions in NFL championship game, 17-16.

1954

9-3—finished first in Eastern Conference. Won NFL championship game, 56-10, against Detroit Lions.

1955

9-2-1—finished first in Eastern Conference. Won NFL championship game, 38-14, against Los Angeles Rams.

1956

5-7—finished fourth in Eastern Conference.

1957

9-2-1—finished first in Eastern Conference. Lost to Detroit Lions in NFL championship game, 59-14.

1958

9-3—Tied New York Giants for Eastern Conference title. Lost to Giants in special playoff, 10-0.

1959

7-5—finished second in Eastern Conference.

1960

8-3-1—finished second in Eastern Conference.

1961

8-5-1—finished third in Eastern Conference.

1962

7-6-1—finished third in Eastern Conference.

1963

10-4—finished second in Eastern Conference.

CLEVELAND BROWNS STATISTICS AND HONORS (CONTD.)

1964

10-3-1—finished first in Eastern Conference. Won NFL championship game, 27-0, against Baltimore Colts.

1965

11-3—finished first in Eastern Conference. Lost to Green Bay Packers in NFL championship game, 23-12.

1966

9-5—finished second in Eastern Conference.

1967

9-5—finished first in Century Division. Lost to Dallas Cowboys in Eastern Conference championship game, 52-14.

1968

10-4—finished first in Century Division. Won Eastern Conference championship game, 31-20, against Dallas Cowboys. Lost to Baltimore Colts in NFL championship game, 34-0.

1969

10-3-1—finished first in Century Division. Won Eastern Conference championship game, 38-14, against Dallas Cowboys. Lost to Minnesota Vikings in NFL championship game, 27-7.

1970

7-7—finished second in American Football Conference (AFC) Central Division.

1971

9-5—finished first in AFC Central Division. Lost to Baltimore Colts in divisional playoff game, 20-3.

1972

10-4—finished second in AFC Central Division. Lost to Miami Dolphins in divisional playoff game, 20-14.

1973

7-5-2—finished third in AFC Central Division.

1974

4-10—finished fourth in AFC Central Division.

1975

3-11—finished fourth in AFC Central Division.

1976

9-5—finished third in AFC Central Division.

1977

6-8—finished fourth in AFC Central Division.

1978

8-8—finished third in AFC Central Division.

1979

9-7—finished third in AFC Central Division.

CLEVELAND BROWNS STATISTICS AND HONORS (CONTD.)

1980

11-5—finished first in AFC Central Division. Lost to Oakland Raiders in divisional playoff game, 14-12.

1981

5-11—finished fourth in AFC Central Division.

1982

4-5—Season was cut short due to player's strike. Lost to Los Angeles Raiders in divisional playoff game, 27-10.

1983

9-7—finished second in AFC Central Division.

1984

5-11—finished third in AFC Central Division.

1985

8-8—finished first in AFC Central Division. Lost to Miami Dolphins in divisional playoff game, 24-21.

1986

12-4—finished first in AFC Central Division. Won divisional playoff game, 23-20, against New York Jets. Lost to Denver Broncos in AFC championship game, 23-20.

1987

10-5—finished first in AFC Central Division. Won divisional playoff game, 38-21, against Indianapolis Colts. Lost to Denver Broncos in AFC championship game, 38-33.

1988

10-6—finished second in AFC Central Division. Lost to Houston Oilers in wild card playoff game, 24-23.

1989

9-6-1—finished first in AFC Central Division. Won divisional playoff game, 34-30, against Buffalo Bills. Lost to Denver Broncos in AFC championship game, 37-21.

1990

3-13—finished fourth in AFC Central Division.

1991

6-10—finished third in AFC Central Division.

1992

7-9—finished third in AFC Central Division.

1993

7-9—finished third in AFC Central Division.

1994

11-5—finished second in AFC Central Division. Won wild card playoff game, 20-13, against New England Patriots. Lost to Pittsburgh Steelers in divisional playoff game, 29-9.

1995

5-11—finished fourth in AFC Central Division.

BROWNS COACHING HISTORY

	Name	W	L	T
1946-62	Paul Brown	167	53	8
1963-70	Blanton Collier	79	38	2
1971-74	Nick Skorich	30	26	2
1975-77	Forrest Gregg	18	23	0
	(Resigned after 13 games in 1977)			
1977	Dick Modzelewski	0	1	0
1978-84	Sam Rutigliano	47	52	0
	(Fired after eight games in 1984)			
1984-88	Marty Schottenheimer	46	31	0
1989-90	Bud Carson	12	14	1
	(Fired after nine games in 1990)			
1990	Jim Shofner	1	7	0
1991-95	Bill Belichick	37	45	0

Cleveland Browns' 1952 coaching staff included (from left to right) Howard Brinker, Blanton Collier, Paul Brown, Weeb Ewbank and Fritz Heisler.

INDIVIDUAL RECORDS

SCORING

Career	Points	Season	Points	Year
Lou Groza	1,608	Jim Brown	126	1965
Don Cockroft	1,080	Leroy Kelly	120	1968
Jim Brown	756	Lou Groza	115	1964
Matt Bahr	677	Matt Stover	113	1995
Leroy Kelly	540	Matt Stover	110	1994
Matt Stover	480	Lou Groza	108	1953
Gary Collins	420	Jim Brown	108	1958
Dante Lavelli	372	Jim Brown	108	1962
Ray Renfro	330	Matt Bahr	104	1988
Kevin Mack	324	Matt Bahr	101	1983

RUSHING

Career	Yards	Season	Yards	Year
Jim Brown	12,312	Jim Brown	1,863	1963
Leroy Kelly	7,274	Jim Brown	1,544	1965
Mike Pruitt	6,540	Jim Brown	1,527	1958
Greg Pruitt	5,496	Jim Brown	1,446	1964
Kevin Mack	5,123	Jim Brown	1,408	1961
Marion Motley	4,712	Jim Brown	1,329	1959
Earnest Byner	3,364	Mike Pruitt	1,294	1979
Ernie Green	3,204	Jim Brown	1,257	1960
Bobby Mitchell	2,297	Leroy Kelly	1,239	1968
Cleo Miller	2,286	Leroy Kelly	1,205	1967

GREATEST SINGLE-GAME RUSHING PERFORMANCE:

Jim Brown	237	November 24, 1957 vs. Los Angeles Rams
Jim Brown	237	November 19, 1961 vs. Philadelphia Eagles

Best Regards
Frank
Sincerly,
Lou Groza

Lou Groza
TACKLE

Lou Groza

PASS RECEIVING (NUMBER):

Career	Number	Season	Number	Year
Ozzie Newsome	662	Ozzie Newsome	89	1983
Dante Lavelli	386	Ozzie Newsome	89	1984
Mac Speedie	349	Ozzie Newsome	69	1981
Gary Collins	331	Mac Speedie	67	1947
Greg Pruitt	323	Greg Pruitt	65	1981
Brian Brennan	315	Webster Slaughter	65	1989
Reggie Rucker	310	Webster Slaughter	64	1991
Webster Slaughter	305	Mike Pruitt	63	1980
Eric Metcalf	297	Mike Pruitt	63	1981
Ray Renfro	281	Eric Metcalf	63	1993

GREATEST SINGLE-GAME RECEIVING PERFORMANCE (NUMBER):

Ozzie Newsome—14 catches on October 14, 1984 vs. New York Jets.

PASS RECEIVING (YARDAGE):

Career	Yards	Season	Yards	Year
Ozzie Newsome	7,980	Webster Slaughter	1,236	1989
Dante Lavelli	6,488	Mac Speedie	1,146	1947
Mac Speedie	5,602	Paul Warfield	1,067	1968
Ray Renfro	5,508	Mac Speedie	1,028	1949
Gary Collins	5,299	Ozzie Newsome	1,002	1981
Paul Warfield	5,210	Ozzie Newsome	1,001	1984
Reggie Rucker	4,953	Dave Logan	982	1979
Webster Slaughter	4,834	Ozzie Newsome	970	1983
Dave Logan	4,247	Gary Collins	946	1966
Milt Morin	4,208	Paul Warfield	920	1964

GREATEST SINGLE-GAME RECEIVING PERFORMANCE (YARDAGE):

Mac Speedie—228 yards on November 20, 1949 vs. Brooklyn Dodgers

PASSING (YARDAGE):

Career	Yards	Season	Yards	Year
Brian Sipe	23,713	Brian Sipe	4,132	1980
Otto Graham	23,584	Brian Sipe	3,876	1981
Bernie Kosar	22,314	Bernie Kosar	3,854	1986
Frank Ryan	13,361	Brian Sipe	3,793	1979
Bill Nelsen	9,725	Brian Sipe	3,566	1983
Milt Plum	8,914	Bernie Kosar	3,533	1989
Mike Phipps	7,700	Bernie Kosar	3,487	1991
Vinny Testaverde	7,255	Paul McDonald	3,472	1984
Paul McDonald	5,269	Bernie Kosar	3,033	1987
Jim Ninowski	2,630	Frank Ryan	2,974	1966

GREATEST SINGLE-GAME PASSING PERFORMANCE (YARDAGE):

Bernie Kosar—489 yards on January 3, 1987 vs. New York Jets

PASSING (TOUCHDOWNS):

Career	Number	Season	Number	Year
Otto Graham	174	Brian Sipe	30	1980
Brian Sipe	154	Frank Ryan	29	1966
Frank Ryan	134	Brian Sipe	28	1979
Bernie Kosar	119	Brian Sipe	26	1983
Bill Nelsen	71	Otto Graham	25	1947
Milt Plum	66	Otto Graham	25	1948
Vinny Testaverde	47	Frank Ryan	25	1963
Mike Phipps	40	Frank Ryan	25	1964
Paul McDonald	24	Bill Nelsen	23	1969
Jim Ninowski	20	Bernie Kosar	22	1987

GREATEST SINGLE-GAME PASSING PERFORMANCE (TOUCHDOWN PASSES):
Otto Graham—six on October 14, 1949 vs. Los Angeles Dons

INTERCEPTIONS:

Career	Number	Season	Number	Year
Thom Darden	45	Tom Collela	10	1946
Warren Lahr	44	Thom Darden	10	1978
Clarence Scott	39	Cliff Lewis	9	1948
Tommy James	34	Tommy James	9	1950
Ken Konz	30	Felix Wright	9	1989
Cliff Lewis	30	Eric Turner	9	1994
Bernie Parrish	29	Bobby Franklin	8	1960
Ross Fichtner	27	Jim Shofner	8	1960
Mike Howell	27	Ross Fichtner	8	1966
Hanford Dixon	26	Mike Howell	8	1966
Ben Davis	8	1968		
Thom Darden	8	1974		

GREATEST SINGLE-GAME PERFORMANCE (INTERCEPTIONS):

Tom Collela—3 on November 17, 1946 vs. Chicago Rockets
Tommy James—3 on November 15, 1950 vs. Chicago Cardinals
Tommy James—3 on November 1, 1953 vs. Washington Redskins
Bobby Franklin—3 on December 11, 1960 vs. Chicago Bears
Bernie Parrish—3 on December 3, 1961 vs. Dallas Cowboys
Ross Fichtner—3 on October 23, 1966 vs. Dallas Cowboys
Ron Bolton—3 on November 27, 1977 vs. Los Angeles Rams
Hanford Dixon—3 on December 19, 1982 vs. Pittsburgh Steelers
Frank Minnifield—3 on November 22, 1987 vs. Houston Oilers
Stevon Moore—3 on September 17, 1995 vs. Houston Oilers

PUNT RETURNS:

Career	Avg.	Season	Avg.	Year
Greg Pruitt	11.8	Leroy Kelly	15.6	1965
Bobby Mitchell	11.2	Greg Pruitt	12.9	1974
Eric Metcalf	10.6	Eric Metcalf	12.9	1993
Leroy Kelly	10.5	Ben Davis	12.7	1967
Gerald McNeil	9.6	Ken Carpenter	12.4	1951
Ken Konz	8.2	Bobby Mitchell	11.8	1958
Dino Hall	8.1	Bobby Mitchell	11.7	1961
Brian Brennan	7.9	Gerald McNeil	11.4	1987
Keith Wright	6.0	Greg Pruitt	11.3	1973
Billy Reynolds	5.4	Bobby Mitchell	10.4	1959
Thom Darden	45	Tom Collela	10	1946

KICKOFF RETURNS:

Career	Avg.	Season	Avg.	Year
Greg Pruitt	26.3	Billy Reynolds	29.5	1954
Walter Roberts	25.9	Bo Scott	28.9	1969
Keith Wright	25.2	Greg Pruitt	28.3	1973
Bobby Mitchell	25.0	Walter Roberts	27.5	1964
Billy Lefear	24.4	Greg Pruitt	27.5	1974
Glen Young	23.9	Walter Roberts	27.4	1965
Leroy Kelly	23.5	Charley Scales	27.0	1963
Randy Baldwin	22.8	Randy Baldwin	26.9	1994
Dino Hall	21.1	Bobby Mitchell	26.8	1961
Gerald McNeil	20.3	Keith Wright	26.3	1978

TOP TEN HIGHEST SCORING BROWNS TEAMS:

Points	Year
423	1946
415	1964
410	1947
403	1966
394	1968
391	1986
390	1987
389	1948
363	1965
362	1960

AWARDS AND HONORS:

CLEVELAND BROWNS' PLAYERS SELECTED
FIRST-TEAM ALL-PRO FROM 1946 TO 1995:

1946—Lou Rymkus (T), Bill Willis (G)

1947—Mac Speedie (E), Otto Graham
(QB)

1948—Mac Speedie (E), Otto Graham
(QB), Marion Motley (RB)

1949—Mac Speedie (E), Lou Rymkus
(T), Lou Saban (C), Otto Graham (QB)

1950—Mac Speedie (E), Bill Willis (G),
Marion Motley (RB)

1951—Dante Lavelli (E), Lou Groza
(T), Frank Gatski (C), Otto Gra-
ham (QB), Dub Jones (HB), Len
Ford (DE), Bill Willis (MG),
Tony Adamle (LB), Warren Lahr
(DB)

Mac Speedie
End

Ray Renfro
Halfback

Tom James
Halfback

Sherman Howard
Halfback

ALL-PRO FIRST-TEAM SELECTIONS (CONT'D.)

1952—Mac Speedie (E), Lou Groza (T), Frank Gatski (C), Otto Graham (QB), Len Ford (DE), Bill Willis (MG)

1953—Dante Lavelli (E), Lou Groza (T), Abe Gibron (G), Frank Gatski (C), Otto Graham (QB), Len Ford (DE), Bill Willis (MG), Tommy Thompson (LB), Ken Gorgal (DB)

1954—Lou Groza (T), Otto Graham (QB), Len Ford (DE)

1955—Lou Groza (T), Mike McCormack (T), Abe Gibron (G), Frank Gatski (C), Otto Graham (QB), Fred Morrison (RB), Len Ford (DE), Don Colo (DT), Don Paul (DB)

1956—NONE

1957—Lou Groza (T), Mike McCormack (T), Jim Brown (RB), Don Colo (DT)

1958—Jim Brown (RB), Bob Gain (DT)

1959—Jim Ray Smith (G), Jim Brown (RB), Walt Michaels (LB)

1960—Jim Ray Smith (G), Jim Brown (RB)

1961—Jim Ray Smith (G), Jim Brown (RB)

1962—Jim Ray Smith (G)

1963—Dick Schafrath (T), Jim Brown (RB)

1964—Paul Warfield (E), Dick Schafrath (T), Jim Brown (RB), Jim Houston (LB)

1965—Gary Collins (E), Dick Schafrath (T), Jim Brown (RB), Jim Houston (LB)

1966—Gene Hickerson (G), John Wooten (G), Leroy Kelly (RB)

1967—Gene Hickerson (G), Leroy Kelly (RB)

1968—Paul Warfield (E), Gene Hickerson (G), Leroy Kelly (RB)

1969—Gary Collins (E), Paul Warfield (E), Gene Hickerson (G), Leroy Kelly (RB)

1970—Gene Hickerson (G)

1971—Leroy Kelly (RB)

1972—Don Cockroft (K)

1973—NONE

1974—NONE

1975—NONE

1976—Jerry Sherk (DT)

ALL-PRO FIRST-TEAM SELECTIONS (CONT'D.)

1977—NONE

1978—Thom Darden (S)

1979—Ozzie Newsome (TE)

1980—Joe DeLamielleure (G), Brian Sipe (QB), Lyle Alzado (DE)

1981—NONE

1982—NONE

1983—Chip Banks (LB)

1984—Ozzie Newsome (TE), Clay Matthews (LB)

1985—Bob Golic (DT)

1986—Hanford Dixon (DB)

1987—Hanford Dixon (DB), Frank Minnifield (DB)

1988—Frank Minnifield (DB)

1989—Michael Dean Perry (DT)

1990—Michael Dean Perry (DT)

1991—Michael Dean Perry (DT)

1992—Michael Dean Perry (DT)

1993—Michael Dean Perry (DT), Eric Metcalf (KR)

1994—Eric Turner (S), Eric Metcalf (KR)

1995—NONE

CLEVELAND BROWNS' PLAYERS SELECTED TO THE PRO BOWL TEAMS FROM 1951 TO 1996:

(The year of selection is the one in which the game was played). Example: If a player was selected from the 1950 season, he played in the 1951 Pro Bowl in January of that year. Also, the AAFC did not have any Pro Bowls, so no Browns were selected until Cleveland's entry into the National Football League in 1950.)

1951— Tony Adamle, Otto Graham, Lou Groza, Weldon Humble, Marion Motley, Mac Speedie, Bill Willis

1952—Tony Adamle, Ken Carpenter, Len Ford, Lou Groza, Otto Graham, Dub Jones, Dante Lavelli, Bill Willis

1953—Len Ford, Abe Gibron, Horace Gillom, Otto Graham, Lou Groza, Bill Willis

1954—Len Ford, Abe Gibron, Otto Graham, Lou Groza, Harry Jagade, Tommy James, Dante Lavelli, Ray Renfro

1955—Don Colo, Len Ford, Frank Gatski, Abe Gibron, Otto Graham, Lou Groza, Dante Lavelli

1956—Darrell Brewster, Don Colo, Abe Gibron, Lou Groza, Ken Konz, Fred Morrison

1957—Darrell Brewster, Mike McCormack, Walt Michaels, Don Paul

1958—Jim Brown, Bob Gain, Lou Groza, Mike McCormack, Walt Michaels, Don Paul, Ray Renfro

Marion Motley, Lou Groza, Otto Graham, Frank Gatski, coach Paul Brown and Dante Lavelli (clockwise from top left).

1959—Jim Brown, Don Colo, Bob Gain, Lou Groza, Walt Michaels, Don Paul, Jim Ray Smith

1960—Jim Brown, Bob Gain, Lou Groza, Art Hunter, Walt Michaels, Jim Ray Smith

1961—Jim Brown, Mike McCormack, Bobby Mitchell, Bernie Parrish, Milt Plum, Ray Renfro, Jim Ray Smith

1962—Jim Brown, Bob Gain, Mike McCormack, John Morrow, Milt Plum, Jim Ray Smith

1963—Jim Brown, Galen Fiss, Bob Gain, Bill Glass, Mike McCormack, Jim Ray Smith

1964—Jim Brown, Galen Fiss, Bill Glass, John Morrow, Bernie Parrish, Dick Schafrath

1965—Jim Brown, Bill Glass, Jim Houston, Dick Modzelewski, Frank Ryan, Dick Schafrath, Paul Warfield

1966—Jim Brown, Gary Collins, Gene Hickerson, Jim Houston, Frank Ryan, Dick Schafrath, Paul Wiggin, John Wooten

1967—Johnny Brewer, Gary Collins, Ernie Green, Gene Hickerson, Leroy Kelly, Frank Ryan, Dick Schafrath, John Wooten

1968—Bill Glass, Ernie Green, Gene Hickerson, Walter Johnson, Leroy Kelly, Milt Morin, Dick Schafrath, Paul Wiggin

1969—Erich Barnes, Gene Hickerson, Walter Johnson, Ernie Kellermann, Leroy Kelly, Milt Morin, Dick Schafrath, Paul Warfield

1970—Jack Gregory, Gene Hickerson, Fred Hoaglin, Jim Houston, Walter

Johnson, Leroy Kelly, Bill Nelsen, Paul Warfield

1971—Gene Hickerson, Jim Houston, Leroy Kelly

1972—Leroy Kelly, Milt Morin

1973—NONE

1974—Greg Pruitt, Clarence Scott, Jerry Sherk

1975—Greg Pruitt, Jerry Sherk

1976—Jerry Sherk

1977—Greg Pruitt, Jerry Sherk

1978—Greg Pruitt

1979—Thom Darden

1980—Tom DeLeone, Mike Pruitt

1981—Joe DeLamielleure, Tom DeLeone, Doug

Dieken, Mike Pruitt, Brian Sipe

Frank Minnifield

1982—Ozzie Newsome

1983—Chip Banks

1984—Chip Banks

1985—Ozzie Newsome

1986—Chip Banks, Bob Golic, Kevin Mack, Clay

Matthews, Ozzie Newsome

1987—Chip Banks, Hanford Dixon, Bob Golic,

Frank Minnifield, Cody Risien

Bob Golic

PRO BOWL SELECTIONS (CONT'D.)

1988—Hanford Dixon, Bob Golic, Bernie Kosar, Kevin Mack, Clay Matthews, Gerald McNeil, Frank Minnifield, Cody Risien

1989—Hanford Dixon, Clay Matthews, Frank Minnifield

Eric Metcalf

1990—Mike Johnson, Clay Matthews, Frank Minnifield, Michael Dean Perry, Webster Slaughter

1991—Mike Johnson, Michael Dean Perry

1992—Michael Dean Perry

1993—NONE

1994—Eric Metcalf, Michael Dean Perry

1995—Rob Burnett, Leroy Hoard, Pepper Johnson, Eric Metcalf, Michael Dean Perry, Eric Turner

1996—NONE

CLEVELAND BROWNS WHO WON MOST VALUABLE PLAYER AWARDS (1946—1995): MOST VALUABLE PLAYER AWARD—PRO BOWL

1951—Otto Graham

1962—Jim Brown

1963—Jim Brown

1966—Jim Brown

ALL-AMERICA FOOTBALL CONFERENCE MVP

1947—Otto Graham

1948—Otto Graham shared award with Frankie Albert of San Francisco

NATIONAL FOOTBALL LEAGUE MVP—FOLLOWING THE PLAYER'S NAME IS THE ORGANIZATION THAT VOTED HIM THEIR MOST VALUABLE PLAYER

1951—Otto Graham—United Press

1953—Otto Graham—United Press

1954—Lou Groza—The Sporting News

1955—Otto Graham—United Press, Sporting News

1957—Jim Brown—Associated Press, Sporting News

1958—Jim Brown—United Press, Associated Press, Newspaper Enterprise,
    Sporting News

1963—Jim Brown—United Press, Newspaper Enterprise, Maxwell Club

1965—Jim Brown—United Press, Associated Press, Sporting News, Newspaper
    Enterprise

1968—Leroy Kelly—Maxwell Club

1980—Brian Sipe—Football Writer's, Associated Press, Sporting News

UNITED PRESS OFFENSIVE PLAYER OF THE YEAR

1980—Brian Sipe

UNITED PRESS AFC DEFENSIVE PLAYER OF THE YEAR

1989—Michael Dean Perry

ROOKIE OF THE YEAR

1957—Jim Brown—United Press, Associated Press, Sporting News

DEFENSIVE ROOKIE OF THE YEAR

1982—Chip Banks—Associated Press, Pro Football Weekly

COACH OF THE YEAR

1951—Paul Brown—*Sporting News*

1953—Paul Brown—United Press, *Sporting News*

1957—Paul Brown—United Press

1976—Forrest Gregg—Associated Press

1979—Sam Rutigliano—United Press AFC Coach of the Year

1980—Sam Rutigliano—United Press AFC Coach of the Year

1986—Marty Schottenheimer—United Press AFC Coach of the Year

PLAYERS WHO HAD THEIR NUMBERS RETIRED BY THE CLEVELAND BROWNS ORGANIZATION:

Number	Name
14	Otto Graham
32	Jim Brown

45	Ernie Davis
46	Don Fleming
76	Lou Groza

CLEVELAND BROWNS FIRST-ROUND DRAFT PICKS (1950–1995, 1999)

1950—Ken Carpenter—Running Back, Oregon State

1951—Ken Konz—Defensive Back, Louisana State

1952—Bert Rechichar— Defensive Back, Tennessee, and Harry Agganis—Quarterback, Boston U.

1953—Doug Atkins—Defensive End, Tennessee

1954—Bobby Garrett—Quarterback, Stanford, and John Bauer—Guard, Illinois

1955—Kurt Burris—Center, Oklahoma

1956—Preston Carpenter—Running Back, Arkansas

1957—Jim Brown—Running Back, Syracuse

1958—Jim Shofner—Defensive Back, Texas Christian

1959—Rich Kreitling—Defensive End, Illinois

1960—Jim Houston—Defensive End, Ohio State

1961—Bobby Crespino—Tight End, Mississippi

1962—Gary Collins—Receiver, Maryland, and Leroy Jackson—Running Back, Western Illinois

1963—Tom Hutchinson—Receiver, Kentucky

1964—Paul Warfield—Receiver, Ohio State

1965—James Garcia—Tackle, Purdue

1966—Milt Morin—Tight End, Massachusetts

1967—Bob Matheson—Linebacker, Duke

1968—Marvin Upshaw—Defensive Tackle, Trinity, Texas

1969—Ron Johnson—Running Back, Michigan

1970—Mike Phipps—Quarterback, Purdue, and Bob McKay—Tackle, Texas

1971—Clarence Scott—Defensive Back, Kansas State

1972—Thom Darden—Defensive Back, Michigan

1973—Steve Holden—Receiver, Arizona State, and Pete Adams—Tackle, Southern California

1974—Billy Corbett—Tackle, Johnson C. Smith

1975—Mack Mitchell—Defensive End, Houston

1976—Mike Pruitt—Running Back, Purdue

1977—Robert Jackson—Linebacker, Texas A&M

1978—Clay Matthews—Linebacker, Southern California, and Ozzie Newsome—Tight End, Alabama

1979—Willis Adams—Receiver, Houston

1980—Charles White—Running Back, Southern California

1981—Hanford Dixon—Defensive Back, Southern Mississippi

1982—Chip Banks—Linebacker, Southern California

1983—Ron Brown—Receiver, Arizona State

1984—Don Rogers—Defensive Back, UCLA (University of California, Los Angeles)

1985—Greg Allen—Running Back, Florida State

1986—Webster Slaughter—Receiver, San Diego State

1987—Mike Junkin—Linebacker, Duke

1988—Clifford Charlton—Linebacker, Florida

1989—Eric Metcalf—Running Back, Texas

1990—Leroy Hoard—Running Back, Michigan

1991—Eric Turner—Defensive Back, UCLA (University of California, Los Angeles)

1992—Tommy Vardell—Running Back, Stanford

1993—Steve Everitt—Center, Michigan

1994—Antonio Langham—Defensive Back, Alabama, and Derrick Alexander—Receiver, Michigan

1995—Craig Powell—Linebacker, Ohio State

1999—Tim Couch—Quarterback, Kentucky

BIBLIOGRAPHY

BOOKS

Brown, Jim with Delsohn, Steve. (1989). *Out of Bounds.* New York: Kensington Publishing Corp.

Brown, Paul with Clary, Jack. (1980). *PB: The Paul Brown Story.* New York: Atheneum.

Byrne, Steve with Campbell, Jim, & Craig, Mark. (1995). *The Cleveland Browns: A 50-year Tradition.* Champaign, IL: Sagamore Publishing.

Clary, Jack. (1973). *Cleveland Browns.* New York: Macmillan Publishing Co., Inc.

Clary, Jack. (1989). *Pro Football's Great Moments.* New York: Bonanza Books.

Clary, Jack. (1983). *Pro Football's Great Moments.* New York: Bonanza Books.

Elias Sports Bureau (Bob Carroll, Michael Gersham, David Neft, John Thorn). (1997). *Total Football: The Official Encyclopedia of the National Football League.* New York: Harper Collins.

Groza, Lou. (1996). *The Toe: The Lou Groza Story.* Dubuque, IA: Kendall/Hunt Publishing Co.

Hollander, Zander. (1969). *Great Moments in Pro Football.* New York: Random House.

Levy, Bill. (1981). *Sam, Sipe, & Company.* Cleveland, OH: J.T. Zubel & P.D. Dole, Publishers.

Neft, David, S. with Cohen, Richard M. & Korch, Rick. (1997). *The Sports Encyclopedia: Pro Football.* (15th ed). New York: St. Martin's Griffin.

Sullivan, George. (1972). *The Great Running Backs.* New York: G.P. Putnam's Sons.

NEWSPAPERS:

The Cleveland Plain Dealer—1946 to 1999

The Cleveland Press—1960 to 1965

OTHERS:

Cleveland Browns Fan and Media Guide

ABOUT THE AUTHOR

Originally from Maple Heights, Ohio, Richard Shmelter now resides in Sagamore Hills, Ohio, with his wife, Helen. Rich is employed by Cleveland Electric Laboratories in Twinsburg, Ohio, and has been a long-time follower of sports history, with special emphasis on pro football. His other interests besides writing are weight-lifting and jogging. This is his first book.

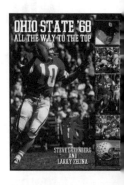

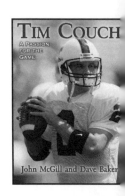

ADDITIONAL TITLES FROM SPORTS PUBLISHING INC.

Lou Boudreau: Covering All the Bases

by Lou Boudreau with Russell Schneider

Lou Boudreau: Covering All the Bases is the personal history of one of the most extraordinary men in baseball history. While leading the Cleveland Indians to a World Series victory in 1948, he invented the "Ted Williams shift," and became the only player/manager ever to win the American League MVP award. His illustrious playing career culminated in 1970, when he was voted into the Baseball Hall of Fame. Boudreau managed the Boston Red Sox, the Kansas City Athletics and the Chicago Cubs before joining WGN as a broadcaster for the Chicago Cubs where he remained for 30 years.

1993 • 203 pp • 8-page b/w photo section • 6 x 9 hardcover • ISBN 0-915611-72-4 • $24.95
(all copies autographed by Hall of Famer Lou Boudreau)

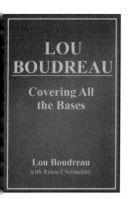

Lou Boudreau: Covering all the Bases ($59.95)

Limited leatherbound edition of 500

Signed by: **Lou Boudreau**
              Bob Feller

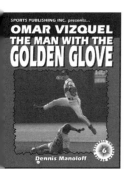

OMAR VIZQUEL: THE MAN WITH THE GOLDEN GLOVE

by Dennis Manoloff

When people talk about the many star players in Major League Baseball today, huge home run numbers often come to mind first. While putting runs on the board is the name of the game, preventing runs can make a player just as valuable to his team. Such has been the case for veteran Cleveland shortstop Omar Vizquel, who has provided his team with solid play and leadership, not to mention multiple Gold Glove Awards. Vizquel's defense has been pivotal to the Indians' success throughout this decade, and helped lead them to the World Series in 1995 and 1997 and the 1998 American League Championship Series.

In *The Man with the Golden Glove* Dennis Manoloff profiles the player that many consider to be the finest defensive shortstop in baseball today. In the book, Vizquel talks about his career and how he was able to make himself into such a great player. He also tells the story of his life growing up in Venezuela, and how baseball played a key role in his development as a person. Vizquel has been one of the main elements behind Cleveland's rise into one of baseball's top organizations, despite the tough losses the team has faced in the post-season.

1999 • 96 pages • 25 b/w photos • 5 1/2 x 7, paperback • ISBN: 1-58261-045-2 • $4.95

**To Order: Call 1-877-424-BOOK (2665) or
e-mail at www.sportspublishinginc.com**